CHEERS AND SKOAL!

Clearly written, comprehensive, with a selection
of drink recipes that range from the Bloody Mary
to a tasty concoction first mixed at the 1933 Chicago
World's Fair, *Harvey Collins' Drink Guide* gives
you all the know-how you need to produce mixed
drinks certain to both please your guests and im-
prove your own appreciation of the cocktail. Sweet
drinks, smooth traditional favorites, summer chillers
and winter warmers, nonalcoholic drinks for the
kids... this book has them all. The recipes include garnish and glassware suggestions as well as
possible substitutions and variations. Short of hir-
ing a professional bartender or going to bartending
school yourself, you won't find a better guide to
the precise and delightful art of good drink mixing
than...

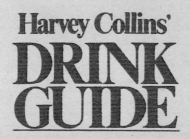

Harvey Collins'
DRINK GUIDE

ATTENTION: SCHOOLS AND CORPORATIONS

WARNER books are available at quantity discounts with bulk purchase for educational, business, or sales promotional use. For information, please write to: SPECIAL SALES DEPARTMENT, WARNER BOOKS, 666 FIFTH AVENUE, NEW YORK, N.Y. 10103.

**ARE THERE WARNER BOOKS
YOU WANT BUT CANNOT FIND IN YOUR LOCAL STORES?**

You can get any WARNER BOOKS title in print. Simply send title and retail price, plus 50¢ per order and 50¢ per copy to cover mailing and handling costs for each book desired. New York State and California residents add applicable sales tax. Enclose check or money order only, no cash please, to: WARNER BOOKS, P.O. BOX 690, NEW YORK, N.Y. 10019.

Harvey Collins'
DRINK GUIDE

WARNER BOOKS

A Warner Communications Company

WARNER BOOKS EDITION

Copyright © 1985 by Harvey Collins
All rights reserved.

All glassware on front cover courtesy of The Pottery Barn, New York City
Cover design by Barbara Buck
Cover photo by Jerry and Nancy Palubniak
Designed by Nicola Mazzella
Text illustrations copyright © 1985 by Lynne Arany

Warner Books, Inc.
666 Fifth Avenue
New York, N.Y. 10103

 A Warner Communications Company

Printed in the United States of America

First Printing: December, 1985

10 9 8 7 6

THANK YOU TO THE FOLLOWING:

Angostura aromatic bitters
Terri Arden
Mindy Bass - Gullivers - Chicago, Ill.
Tom Carney
Robert Cohan
Jean Cohan
Scott Colia
Karen, Andrea, Christine, Susan, Adam and Elizabeth Cohan
Dana Hutchinson - Ranalli's Off Rush
Rebecca Mitchell
Joni Nugent
Johnnie Unger - Myron & Phil, Lincolnwood, Ill.
Ron Vecchione - P.O.E.T.S. - Chicago, Ill.

INTRODUCTION

This book is intended for anyone with an interest in serving alcoholic beverages for pleasure. If we accomplish nothing more than to make you comfortable and fearless when preparing drinks, this book will have served its primary purpose. Most people have the idea that mixing drinks, especially "exotic" drinks, is difficult. The fear of being made to look foolish or inept prevents the relaxation and joy that should easily be attainable by following the simple directions of this guide.

My grandfather, father, and uncle founded Collins Brothers, Inc., in 1934. We are producers and distributors of "everything for the liquor retailer except the liquor." We directly import corkscrews, bota bags (wineskins), wine racks, etc. We distribute glassware, olives, cherries, etc. Most importantly, we produce to our own formula Collins Sweet Sour Mix, Stone Sour Mix, Watermelon Mix, Kamikaze Mix, Long Island Iced Tea Mix, Grenadine, Lemon and Lime Spray, Bar Syrup, Coco Collins Cream of Coconut, Cherry Juice, Margarita Salt, and cans of Bar Sugar. These items are under the Collins label. We also distribute such recommended products as Angostura Aromatic Bitters, Rose's Lime Juice, Mr. & Mrs. T Bloody Mary Mix, and others.

The above may reflect upon my objectivity in the suggestions that follow. There is definitely a bias or pre-disposition in promoting these items. But the end result will be mutually advantageous. For example, Collins Sweet Sour premix is definitely what you should use. It is a good value, contains a foamy-head ingredient, and the taste is perfect.

Even if you cannot find Collins Sweet Sour premix, a substitute sweet-sour should be available. If it meets the test of making good drinks, being economical (it does not take ½ the bottle to make a single drink), and it has a foamy-head ingredient—buy it!

This bears repeating—a good sweet-sour premix is an indispensable item for your bar. The convenience, ease of use, and uniformly good-tasting drinks make it a mainstay of the bar.

Take your own survey and confirm that almost every bartender uses a sweet-sour premix as a basic ingredient. Ask at your favorite bar or restaurant and the answer will be a private-label sweet-sour premix. As a matter of fact, many of the bartenders interviewed in writing this book were unable to produce a scratch sweet-sour because they have relied for so long on a premix.

Why dwell on a sweet-sour premix? Simply because I deem it essential to a bar. A good premix has the proper lemon-lime balance (between tart and sweet), it has dissolved the sugar, which is very difficult to dissolve in liquor, and finally, it has a foamy-head ingredient. It will give uniformly good results with ease, and it will save you money and mess.

The only excuse for not using a sweet-sour premix is that you prefer the taste of fresh ingredients and enjoy the labor when mixing a few drinks. (One word of caution. When using egg white in a scratch mix, it will only remain usable for at most 24 hours, even if refrigerated.)

The last word on any premix, whether it is a sweet-sour or a watermelon mix, is taste. Experiment by yourself prior to any party with the drinks you want to make. You should enjoy the results before you serve anyone else. There are some mixes on the market that are terrible. Experiment, find a good label, and then stay with it.

There are nonalcoholic premixes that require you to add the liquor, and some of these are quite good. They come in three forms: liquid, dry, and freezable buckets. You should experiment with some of these (especially if it is a difficult drink to make from scratch). You can also vary the amount of liquor to make it more palatable. Sometimes the premixes call for too much liquor.

One reason we developed Collins Long Island Iced Tea Mix was the difficulty most people had in mixing the many liquors to obtain the proper taste. It also required that you have five different liquors. Using our mix, only one liquor (vodka) is necessary, and the results are uniformly excellent. It saves time and money and enables you to be confident in the end result.

In the next section—Stocking Your Bar—you will find that only two basic premixes are required—sweet-sour and a mild Bloody Mary mix. These are as essential to any bar as vodka.

Stocking Your Bar

Before buying the liquor for your bar, glance through the recipes in this book. Determine what sounds good to you.

For a basic bar the following are necessary:

Vodka
Bourbon whiskey
Bacardi rum

Gin
Scotch
Tequila
Southern Comfort
Kahlúa
Bailey's Irish Cream
Vermouth (small bottle)
Triple Sec (small bottle)
Amaretto
Brandy or cognac (Spanish brandy is good
    and not expensive)
White wine
Beer
Angostura (4 oz. size)
Rose's lime juice (7 oz. size)
Bar syrup (liquid sugar, Collins label)
Mild Bloody Mary premix
Sweet-sour premix (Collins label)
#8 queen olives (one jar, Collins label)
Whole stem cherries (8 oz. jar, Collins
    label)
Grenadine (12 oz. size, Collins label)
Tomato juice
Orange juice
Fresh lemons and limes
Margarita salt (Collins label)
Club soda
Ginger ale
7-Up

Squirt
Cola
Fresh—store bought, clear, clean,
  odorless—ice cubes

Utensils

The following will simplify the proper operation of your bar. It will also make you feel comfortable. Use this as a checklist before any large gathering.

Wing corkscrew or waiter's corkscrew with
  a sharp knife
2 can openers
Cutting board or surface for cutting
Cocktail shaker and fitting glass (even a
  3-piece plastic shaker)
Bar spoon
Good sharp knife
Jigger—1½ by ¾ oz. Generally the size
  is imprinted on each end of the jigger.
  There are also easy-to-use see-through
  plastic jiggers or measuring glasses.
Cocktail napkins and coasters
Blender
Ice bucket and ice tongs

Pitcher for water and another for mixes
Strainer
Measuring spoons
Muddler
Plastic picks, sip sticks, stir rods—Collins
    brand
Towels

Corkscrews

Waiter's with knife. This is excellent. It should be sturdy with a knife. The best are Italian and French. The waiter's cork- 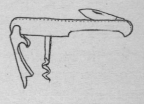 screw without a knife is cheaper because of im- port duty. Buy a good one with a knife.

Two-prong cork-puller. This corkscrew has two thin metal prongs. The tips of the prongs are placed inside the bottle on either side of the cork. A gentle rocking motion pushes the prongs in, and a gentle pulling and twisting extracts the cork. This is a good way to remove the cork completely without cork particles being left in the bottle. Can also be used to recork the bottle with a reverse action.

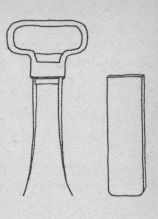

Wing corkscrew or lever corkscrew. This is the most popular corkscrew and probably the one you should use at your bar. Make sure you buy the Italian wing corkscrew and not one made in the Orient. Also, purchase it in chrome, not brass. Brass tarnishes too easily. There are two types of ferrules. The most popular is the

machine-made which is one piece and flat. The other is a wire worm, which is less popular, but some think it is superior in that it does not shred the cork as much as the machine screw.

Regular corkscrew. Another popular corkscrew is the "regular" corkscrew. It has a wooden handle and the ferrule is machine-made. It is durable and inexpensive. (Collins Brothers imports them from Italy.)

Power corkscrew. The power corkscrew has a wooden handle with a bell-like bracket at the top of the machine screw. The bell contacts the top of the bottle and starts the cork out automatically.

The above are the most popular corkscrews. There are many others such as two-piece wood and plastic corkscrews. These are generally sheathed, inexpensive, and portable.

Glassware

There are basically two ways of manufacturing glassware—hand-blown and machine. The difference is obvious when the two are compared. The hand-blown glass is thin and beautiful. However, it is expensive and easily breakable. Machine-made glass is durable and more reasonably priced.

The difficulty of this section is that to properly stock a bar with glassware takes an incredible amount of space and expense. Thus, it is my suggestion to have eight glasses each of the following shapes:

FLUTED CHAMPAGNE
TALL WINEGLASS
6 OZ. BRANDY SNIFTER
OLD-FASHIONED GLASS
COCKTAIL GLASS
2 OZ. SHOT GLASS
COLLINS GLASS

Fluted champagne but not a hollow stem. The hollow stem is attractive but very difficult to clean. In some areas it is illegal to use hollow-stem glasses in bars, restaurants, or other public places. The flute shape is better than a saucer bowl in that it will preserve the bubbles and aroma. It takes longer for the effervescence to fade in a flute shape.

The second glass is a *tall wineglass* with at least a 10 oz. capacity. (Also used for Bloody Marys, Piña Coladas, etc.)

6 oz. brandy snifter is used for cordials, straight shots, as well as for brandy. It is never filled to the top!

A heavy 10 to 15 oz. *old-fashioned glass* for "on the rocks" drinks.

A straight-up *cocktail glass* for Martinis, Margaritas, etc. Six-oz. size is best.

The next glass is a *2 oz. shot glass* without a line.

Lastly, a tall, unfrosted *Collins glass*. The reason for not wanting the traditional frosted Collins glass is the belief that being able to see the finished drink adds to its enjoyment.

Purchasing 8 of each of these glasses requires plenty of room and is not inexpensive. However, if you need to reduce the variety, why not cut out the Collins glass and use the tall wineglass as its replacement. The stem glass requires no coaster and keeps the drink colder as long as it is only held by the stem and not by the bowl.

In the event that more than 8 glasses of each size are needed, you can rent glassware. Also, today for some parties it is common to use plastic disposable tumblers. It is even generally permissible to use translucent soft plastic cups at larger gatherings. In any event, it is best to use only clear, undecorated glass so that the beauty of the drink will be easily seen.

Planning A Party

This is not going to be a detailed discussion. You will find only the basics.

Invitations. It is best to invite by written invitation. Let the guest RSVP only with regrets. It is not in the best taste to invite more than two weeks before a party. This does not allow a graceful way for the guest to decline.

A written invitation also provides a ready refresher as to the time and date and does away with uncertainty. It also shows effort and thought on your part. It will provide you with an opportunity to scan your list to make certain that people who will be uncomfortable with each other are excluded, such as an ex–girl friend or ex-husband.

Take a few moments to determine traffic patterns in your home. It may be a good idea to set the bar up in one area and the food in another. People tend to congregate at these places, and you thus avoid crowding.

What is the most comfortable pattern for your home? Where will coats be stored? How will seating be arranged? It may be wise to have food in two or three areas. Some thought on your part prior to the party can be extremely useful.

Is your party going to have a theme drink such as Piña Coladas, Margaritas, or Bloody Marys? You should decide prior to the party. If it's a large party, you should plan only 2 mixed drinks. These should be served by the pitcher. The remaining mixed drinks should be simple drinks with water or on the rocks. A guest is rude if he requests a difficult mixed drink at a large gathering unless you have a professional bartender.

If possible, take note of the liquor and drinks consumed by the same people at a previous party. For example, we often attend a Christmas party with substantially the same people we invite to our New Year's Eve party. Be observant and determine what was consumed. This information will be invaluable as to the amount and types of liquor and mixes you will need.

Responsibility

This issue must be raised. You have a legal and moral responsibility for your guests and their consumption of alcohol.

Common sense can avoid a tragedy. It is your responsibility as a friend or just as a host to protect your guests from overindulging. Moderation in all things may seem trite, but too many people are killed and maimed by drunks.

You must watch your guests and decide when they have had enough. Be sure to serve food to blunt some of the effects of the drinking. Be careful of anyone on medication or who seems "under the weather." The consequences of an error are so grave that if a mistake is made, make it on the side of caution and prohibit that person from any further alcohol. I will not invite someone who is troublesome to a party. Offer coffee at the end of the party. It will not sober anyone up, but time will. Lastly, *drive or have someone drive* an inebriated person home.

Even as a serving host, you must be free to roam and enjoy your own party. Your enjoyment will be contagious. It is also your function to relax guests who are hesitant to request a second drink and to assist them in mixing with other people at the party.

You will notice that the section dealing with stocking your bar suggests nonalcoholic mixes. These should be available to anyone who does not want to consume liquor.

Tips

Hangover remedy. Supposedly no remedy exists, but the following has been sworn to as effective by a great bartender.

Upon awakening with a hangover, go to the kitchen. Do not eat or drink anything except 2 pieces of white bread which have been toasted dark. Do not have any liquid at all. You should be feeling better within 15 minutes.

Ice

One of the most important ingredients in any drink or bar is ice. Buy commercial ice cubes in greater quantities than you can use. The only limitation on this is storage space. The freezer may not have enough room, but you may have a foam summer cooler. This is an excellent and inexpensive way to store ice for a few hours. (Collins Brothers also sells foam coolers.)

Ice stored or made in the refrigerator absorbs any odor that is present in the refrigerator. There are tricks such as running warm water over cloudy cubes, etc. It's not worth the bother. Buy more commercial ice cubes than you believe are needed.

Always chill the glass and the ingredients before serving. This preserves the ice in the drink much longer. Remember ice, as it melts, dilutes the drink. An average ice cube contains between 1 and 1½ oz. of water.

Because ice dilutes a drink and changes its taste, you do not want to stir or shake a drink with ice in it any longer than absolutely necessary.

A block of ice such as is used in a punch keeps longest. Crushed ice will dissolve faster than cubes, and shaved ice will dissolve quickest of all. The larger the piece of ice, the slower it dissolves. The prechilled glass and ingredients will retard the loss of the ice.

Block ice may be made by taking a cube tray and removing the divider. You can also cut a milk container in half and use it to make a block of ice.

To make crushed ice, use a towel and a mallet (hammer).

Ice should generally be placed in the glass or shaker first before adding the liquor. Use ice cubes for highballs or drinks served on the rocks. When using a blender or shaker, you should use crushed or cracked ice. You must have clear, odorless ice.

Flaming drinks

There is not a single recipe in this guide for a flaming drink. They are beautiful and hold a certain mystique, but they are simply too dangerous. Even experienced professionals have had serious accidents with flaming drinks. The flame is sometimes so faint as to be barely seen. On occasion, it has traveled back to the bottle, turning it into a Molotov cocktail. Flaming a drink is just not worth the danger.

Measuring

Always measure accurately when making a drink. A heavy hand will spoil the drink and cause unwanted inebriation in your guest. Measuring also saves liquor.

Pouring

When you are pouring 3 or more mixed drinks, you want each to be uniform. Line the glasses up, placing their rims together in a row. Pour into each glass until each one is ½ filled. Then return to the first glass and completely fill it. This way, each drink has an equal consistency rather than just the lightest or heaviest part of the mixture.

Lemons and Limes

A lemon twist is the skin of the lemon. It should be cut in small pieces about 1 inch long and ¼ inch wide. Use only the colored surface of the peel. The oil of both the lemon and the lime is in the skin. This is the area that also contains the distinctive aroma and taste.

Storage of the lemon peel is difficult, but the following works: Wrap the peels in a wet napkin and then place the napkin into a glass container and store in the refrigerator.

For storing wedges or fruit, put it into a dry glass and put a wet napkin over the top of the glass.

When the recipe calls for a lemon twist, rub the lemon peel around the rim of the glass, then twist the peel over the drink and drop the peel into the drink. The twisting of the peel releases its oil into the drink. It adds a delightful smell and taste.

You can test the theory that twisting releases the oil by *very* carefully twisting a lemon peel over a candle. Twist the peel from well above the candle and it will cause a small explosion.

Chill Your Glass and Ingredients

This is possibly one of our most important tips. A chilled glass along with chilled ingredients keeps ice from diluting and keeps a great drink great.

To chill a glass quickly, fill it with ice and let it stand for a few minutes. Shake the ice and water out of the glass. Normally, if you have time and space, put the glasses in your refrigerator and/or freezer.

Salt Rim of Glass

This is simple. Moisten the glass rim with lemon or lime juice and dip the rim of the glass into salt. Hold the glass upside down so the stem does not get soiled by the juice. The salt should be coarse. Use Collins Margarita Salt, as the container is perfect for dipping and the salt is coarse. Make sure the rim of the glass is equally covered with juice and dipped so the salt will also be even.

Float

To float cream or liquor on top of a drink, invert a spoon. Hold the inverted spoon inside the glass but just above the liquid. Pour the cream or liquor on the rounded bottom of the spoon very slowly.

Stirring

Carbonated drinks should not be stirred hard or long, as they will go flat. Stirring keeps a clear drink clear, while shaking makes a drink cloudy. Shaking produces a colder, more diluted drink than does stirring, provided ice is used.

Proof

Proof, on the label, is the alcohol content in a bottle. It is arrived at by doubling the percentage of alcohol. Thus, 100 proof means there is 50 percent alcohol. Ninety proof means 45 percent alcohol, etc.

To Make a Frozen Drink

Blend with lots of ice for a longer time than usual. You should have more ice than liquid to begin with, but you may have to add more liquor. For example, in a strawberry daiquiri you may have to add more strawberry liqueur, as the making of a frozen drink deprives the drink of some of its flavor.

How to Separate an Egg

Break the egg in half. Pass the yolk back and forth between the 2 shells. Place a bowl under the shells. The egg white will fall into the bowl while the yolk is being passed back and forth. If the egg white is being used as a foamer, it will only keep a short time, even when refrigerated.

Wine

Instead of deciphering wine labels or determining good years of wine, etc., I have a simple suggestion. Go to your neighborhood liquor retailer and ask for assistance. Tell him what you like and how much you want to spend. If it is for a dinner party, tell him what you are serving.

You will know what expertise he has after your first conversation. Return to the same person and bring the label of the consumed wine. Tell him if it was too sweet, too dry, etc., and ask him to suggest another bottle.

This approach has proven successful. The only pitfall is the rare instance where the shopkeeper is disinterested. Generally, people find the wine retailer is enthusiastic, helpful, and is interested in saving you money. Because, if you are satisfied, he has a loyal customer. It also gives him the opportunity to use his expertise.

Remember—Enjoy in Moderation

A

ABBEY

1½ oz. gin
¾ oz. orange juice
Dash of orange bitters

Shake well with ice. Strain into a cocktail glass with ice and garnish with a cherry.

ABBY COCKTAIL

1½ oz. gin
½ oz. orange juice
Dash of sweet vermouth
2 dashes of Angostura bitters

Shake well with ice. Strain into a cocktail glass with ice and garnish with a cherry.

ACAPULCO

1¾ oz. rum
¼ oz. Triple Sec
½ oz. lime juice
1 egg white
½ teaspoon superfine sugar
Mint leaves

Combine ingredients and shake well with ice. Strain into a cocktail or old-fashioned glass over ice. Partially tear the mint leaves and drop them into the drink.

ALABAMA FIZZ

3 oz. gin
1 tablespoon superfine sugar
2 tablespoons lemon juice

Combine ingredients and shake well. Strain and pour into a 10 to 14 oz. glass. Fill glass with club soda. Add a sprig of mint.

ALABAMA SLAMMER

¾ oz. Southern Comfort
¾ oz. amaretto
1½ oz. orange juice
¾ oz. bourbon

Combine with ice and serve in a rocks glass.

ALEXANDER

1 oz. gin
½ oz. crème de cacao
½ oz. sweet cream

Blend with shaved ice and strain into a chilled cocktail glass. (Use brandy instead of gin for a Brandy Alexander. Also, rum can be used instead of gin.)

ALLIGATOR OR SWAMP WATER

1½ oz. Midori
4 oz. orange juice

Fill a highball glass with ice, add ingredients, and stir.

ALMOND COLADA

3 oz. amaretto
¼ cup cream of coconut
1½ oz. vodka
1 oz. chocolate syrup

Mix well and serve over ice in an old-fashioned glass.

ALMOND MOCHA

1 cup hot chocolate
1½ oz. amaretto

Use a mug and partially fill it with hot chocolate. (You can use an instant powdered mix.) Add 1½ oz. amaretto and top with whipped cream.

AMARETTO AND CREAM

2 oz. amaretto
1 oz. cream

Mix ingredients with cracked ice in a shaker. Shake well and strain into a cocktail glass. If you prefer, pour the amaretto into an ice-filled rocks glass or empty cordial glass and use an inverted spoon to float the cream on top.

AMARETTO SOUR

1½ oz. amaretto
3 oz. lemon juice

Blend or shake with 1 cup of cracked ice. Pour into an old-fashioned glass or strain into a cocktail glass. Garnish with an orange slice. The lemon juice can be and probably should be replaced by a sweet-sour ready mix such as Collins Sweet Sour. Check the concentration and recipe on any ready mix. Some are 1 to 1 while others are 2 or 3 to 1. A ready mix will also give a foamy head to a drink.

AMARETTO STONE SOUR

1½ oz. amaretto
1½ oz. lemon juice
1½ oz. orange juice

Blend or shake with 1 cup of cracked ice. Pour into an old-fashioned glass or strain into a cocktail glass. Garnish with an orange slice and a cherry.

This recipe can also be changed to a sweet-sour ready mix or even Collins Stone Sour Mix. Again, a premix should contain a foaming ingredient for a foamy head on the drink.

AMERICANO

1½ oz. sweet vermouth
1½ oz. Campari

Fill a rocks glass with ice. Add the vermouth and Campari in equal proportions. It is optional to fill glass with club soda. Garnish with a lemon twist.

ANGEL'S TIP

1½ oz. dark crème de cacao (or 1½ oz. Kahlúa)
¾ oz. cream

Pour the crème de cacao (or Kahlúa) into a large cordial glass. Take a spoon and invert it over the top of the liquid. Pour cream slowly over the back of the spoon and the cream will float on top. Put a pick through a cherry and lay it on top.

APPLE TODDY

1½ oz. apple brandy
Hot apple cider

Pour apple brandy in a coffee mug. Next, pour in heated apple cider to fill the mug. Garnish with a cinnamon stick.

APRICOT CIDER

1½ oz. apricot brandy
Hot apple cider

Combine the brandy and hot cider in a coffee mug. Garnish with a cinnamon stick. This is good for a party as a large batch is easily made up.

APRICOT SOUR

1½ oz. apricot brandy
3 oz. lemon juice

Blend or shake ingredients with 1 cup of cracked ice. Pour into old-fashioned glass or strain into a cocktail glass. Garnish with an orange slice and cherry. (*The lemon juice should be replaced by a liquid sweet-sour ready mix. When using a sweet-sour mix, be sure to check its concentration and recipe. Also, look at the premix to make certain it gives an ingredient for a foamy head. If possible, use a blender, as it makes the drink hold up better and longer.*)

APRICOT STONE SOUR

1½ oz. apricot brandy
1½ oz. sweetened lemon juice
1½ oz. orange juice

Shake or blend with one cup of cracked ice. Pour into an old-fashioned glass or strain into a cocktail glass. Garnish with an orange slice and a cherry. (The sweetened lemon juice can be replaced by a sweet-sour ready mix. The sweetened lemon juice may also be replaced by unsweetened lemon juice. You can also replace both the lemon juice and the orange juice with Collins Stone Sour Mix.)

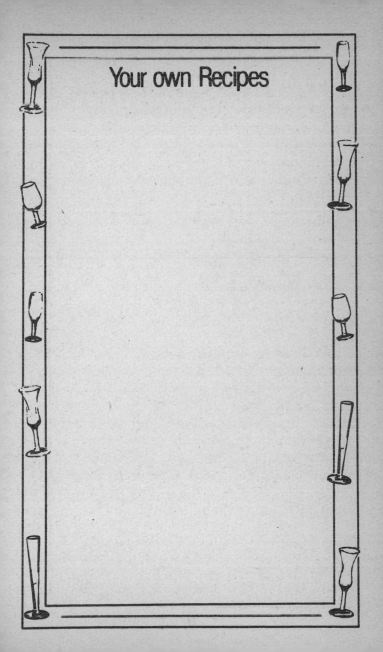

Your own Recipes

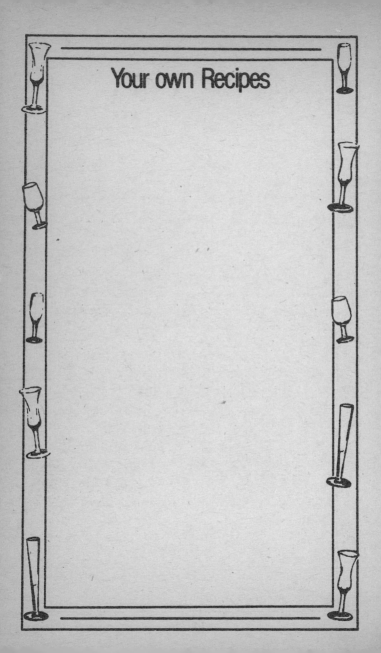

Your own Recipes

B

B&B

1½ oz. Benedictine
½ oz. brandy

Using a cordial glass or preferably a snifter, pour the Benedictine and the brandy together into the glass. This is all the blending that is necessary.

B-52

1 oz. Kahlúa
1 oz. Irish cream
½ oz. cognac

Put the Kahlúa and Irish cream in a rocks glass filled with ice. Invert a spoon and float (pour) the cognac over the spoon on top of the mixed Kahlúa and Irish cream.

B.J.

¾ oz. Kahlúa
¾ oz. amaretto
Whipped cream

Pour liquor into a shot glass. Stir. Rim the shot glass with whipped cream.

BACARDI COCKTAIL

1½ oz. Bacardi rum
1 oz. lemon or lime juice
½ teaspoon grenadine

Combine with cracked ice and shake well. Pour into a rocks glass or strain into a cocktail glass.

BANANA COLADA

1 oz. cream of coconut
1½ oz. rum
½ ripe banana
½ oz. banana liqueur

Combine in a blender with ½ cup of ice. Then serve without garnish in a large stemmed glass.

BANANA DAIQUIRI

1½ oz. rum
2 oz. sweetened lemon juice (or sweet-sour premix)
½ banana, sliced

Put ingredients into a blender with ice. Blend for 30 seconds and pour into a 10 oz. stemmed glass. No garnish. (Optional: You can add ½ oz. cream of banana liqueur.)

BANANA MOCHA

Cup of hot chocolate
1½ oz. banana liqueur

Pour hot chocolate into a coffee mug. Add banana liqueur. Stir and top with whipped cream.

BANSHEE

1 oz. banana liqueur
1 oz. white crème de cacao
1 oz. half-and-half

Put ingredients into a blender for 30 seconds with 1 cup of cracked ice, or fill a cocktail shaker with ice, add ingredients, shake well. Strain into a cocktail glass or champagne glass. No garnish.

SUPER BANSHEE

¾ oz. banana liqueur
¾ oz. white crème de cacao
½ oz. amaretto
¾ oz. half-and-half

Follow the same mixing ingredients as for a Banshee.

BETWEEN THE SHEETS I

1 oz. rum
½ oz. Triple Sec
½ oz. brandy
1 oz. sweetened lemon juice
1 cup cracked ice

Shake ingredients well and pour into a rocks glass or strain and pour into a cocktail glass.

BETWEEN THE SHEETS II

½ oz. cognac
½ oz. dark crème de cacao
½ oz. cream
1 dash of Angostura bitters
1 teaspoon sugar

Shake well and strain into a cocktail glass. Use a lemon peel as a garnish.

BLACKBERRY SOUR

1½ oz. blackberry brandy
1½ oz. lemon juice
Dash Angostura bitters

Blend or shake with 1 cup of cracked ice. Pour into an old-fashioned glass or strain into a cocktail glass. Garnish with an orange slice. (The lemon juice should be replaced by a sweet-sour ready mix such as Collins Sweet Sour. Check the concentrate and recipe on any ready mix. Some are 1 to 1 while others are 2 or 3 to 1. A ready mix will also give a foamy head to a drink.)

BLACK RUSSIAN

1½ oz. vodka
¾ oz. Kahlúa or coffee liqueur

Fill a rocks glass with ice. Add ingredients. Color should be a light brown.

BLACK VELVET

Fill a champagne glass with champagne. Invert a spoon over the champagne. Float brandy on top of the champagne.

BLOOD CLOT (Christine's favorite)

½ oz. Southern Comfort
½ oz. amaretto
¼ oz. grenadine
7-Up

Fill ½ of a rocks glass with 7-Up. Take a shot glass and add Southern Comfort and amaretto. Float the grenadine on top of the shot glass. Put the shot glass inside the rocks glass. Drink together. It should taste like a favorite soft drink.

BLOODY BULL

1½ oz. vodka
2 oz. tomato juice
2 oz. beef bouillon

Season with Tabasco sauce, Worcestershire, lemon juice, celery salt, salt, pepper, and/or horseradish to suit your taste. Fill a highball glass with ice and add the seasoned tomato juice and beef bouillon. Next add the vodka and stir.

BLOODY MARIA

1½ oz. tequila
2 oz. or 4 oz. tomato juice
1 dash Tabasco sauce
1 dash Worcestershire sauce
1 dash lemon juice or lime juice

You may also add celery salt, salt, pepper, and horseradish. First season the tomato juice to taste. Fill a large wineglass, a highball or a Collins glass with ice, then add the tomato juice mix and the tequila. Garnish with a wedge of lime.

BLOODY MARY

1½ oz vodka
2–4 oz. tomato juice

SEASONINGS—Add a dash of any or all of the following as desired.

Tabasco sauce, Worcestershire sauce, lemon juice, celery salt, salt, pepper, horseradish and Angostura bitters.

Fill a highball or Collins glass with ice and add the tomato juice mixture, seasoned to your taste. Next add the vodka. Shake with ice and strain into a glass with ice cubes. Garnish with a wedge of lime and/or a celery stick. Gin may be substituted for vodka.

A Bloody Mary is one of the most popular drinks. I suggest a pitcherful be made before a party and labeled. I also suggest that you experiment with the seasonings in small tastings to determine what blend you find most pleasurable. One suggestion is to make a mild batch and leave the Tabasco sauce, Worcestershire, and salt next to the pitcher. Your guests may be told to use these seasonings themselves to make the drink to their own taste.

Another sensible idea is to use a ready liquid premix. Reading the labels of the premixes will tell you how hot or spicy each mix is attempting to be (for example, "Smooth & Spicy" or "Snap-E-Tom," etc.). I am also suggesting that you experiment with the mixes and choose as mild a premix as possible. If you serve a mild mix, no guest will be unhappy. With seasonings provided, guests may proceed to make their Bloody Marys as hot or as mild as they wish.

BOILERMAKER

Serve 1½ oz. of whiskey straight, in a shot glass. Serve a beer for a chaser.

BOURBON SOUR

1½ oz. bourbon
1 or 2 oz. sweetened lemon juice

Blend or shake with 1 cup of cracked ice. Pour into an old-fashioned glass or strain into a cocktail glass. Garnish with an orange slice. (The sweetened lemon juice can be replaced by a sweet-sour premix such as Collins Sweet Sour. Check the concentrate and recipe on any ready mix. Some are 1 to 1 while others are 2 or 3 to 1. A ready mix will also give a foamy head to a drink.)

If you do not wish to use a sweet-sour premix and you still want a foamy head, you can use 1 egg white or buy a ready-mix foamy head.

BOXCAR

1 oz. gin
½ oz. Cointreau
½ oz. lime juice
1 egg white
Dash of grenadine

Combine with ice and shake ingredients well. Strain and pour into a wine or champagne glass whose rim has been sugar frosted.

BRANDY ALEXANDER

1 oz. brandy
¾ oz. dark crème de cacao
¾ oz. cream or half-and-half

Shake ingredients well in a cocktail shaker and strain into a cocktail or tulip glass. Sprinkle with nutmeg.

BRANDY CIDER

1½ oz. brandy
Hot cider

Using a coffee mug, add ingredients and garnish with a cinnamon stick.

BRANDY COCKTAIL

1½ oz. brandy
½ oz. curaçao
Dash of Angostura bitters

Stir with ice. Strain into a cocktail glass. Garnish with a lemon peel.

BRANDY COLLINS

1½ oz. brandy
1 oz. lemon juice
1 teaspoon fine sugar
Club soda

Blend or shake the brandy and the lemon juice and sugar with ice. Pour into a Collins glass. Top with club soda and garnish with an orange and cherry.

BRANDY FIZZ

2 oz. brandy
½ oz. lemon juice
1 teaspoon superfine sugar
Club soda

Combine ingredients, except club soda, with ice. Shake well or blend. Strain into a chilled tulip glass and add club soda.

Or, after combining ingredients by shaking or blending, pour into an ice-filled highball glass and add club soda.

BRANDY FLIP

2 oz. brandy
1 small egg
1 teaspoon sugar
Grated nutmeg

Shake ingredients (except nutmeg) with ice and strain into a chilled cocktail glass. Sprinkle with the nutmeg.

BRANDY ICE

1 oz. crème de cacao
1 oz. brandy
Two scoops vanilla ice cream

Blend ingredients with crushed ice for 30 seconds in a blender. Serve in a champagne glass.

BRANDY MANHATTAN

2 oz. brandy
½ oz. sweet vermouth
Dash Angostura bitters

Stir with ice and strain into a chilled cocktail glass. For a dry Brandy Manhattan, use dry vermouth. You can also use ¼ oz. sweet vermouth or ¼ oz. dry vermouth. Garnish with a cherry or lemon peel.

BRANDY OLD FASHIONED

2 oz. brandy
3 dashes Angostura bitters
1 teaspoon fine sugar

Stir sugar, bitters, and a teaspoon of water in a chilled old-fashioned glass. Fill the glass with ice cubes and then add the brandy. Stir well and add an orange slice and cherry or even a pineapple chunk. Also, club soda can be used instead of water.

BRANDY SOUR

1½ oz. brandy
1 oz. or 2 oz. lemon juice (to taste)

Blend or shake with 1 cup of cracked ice. Pour into an old-fashioned glass or strain into a cocktail glass. Garnish with an orange slice. The sweetened lemon juice can be replaced by a sweet-sour ready mix such as Collins Sweet Sour. A ready mix will also give a foamy head to a drink.

BRANDY STONE SOUR

1½ oz. brandy
1½ oz. lemon juice
1½ oz. orange juice

Blend or shake with 1 cup of cracked ice. Pour into an old-fashioned glass or strain into a cocktail glass. Garnish with an orange slice and a cherry. This recipe can be changed to a sweet-sour ready mix (watch the concentrate) or Collins Stone Sour Mix. Again, a premix should contain a foaming ingredient for a foamy head on a drink.

BRAVE BULL

1 oz. brandy
¾ oz. coffee liqueur

Using an old-fashioned glass, pour the brandy over ice, then the coffee liqueur.

BULLSHOT

1½ oz. vodka
3 oz. beef bouillon

Fill a highball glass with ice and add vodka. Next add the beef bouillon. Stir and add a lemon twist or mint. Can also be made exactly like a Bloody Mary, except using bouillon or consommé instead of tomato juice. Can use Tabasco, Worcestershire sauce, etc.

BUN WARMER

¾ oz. apricot brandy
¾ oz. Southern Comfort
Hot cider

Add the brandy and Southern Comfort in a coffee mug. Fill the mug with hot cider. Garnish with a cinnamon stick.

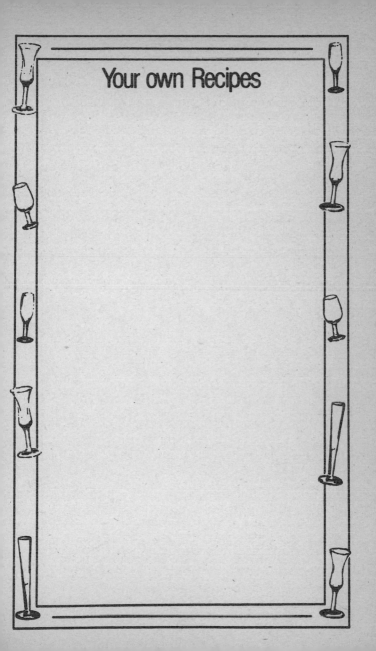

Your own Recipes

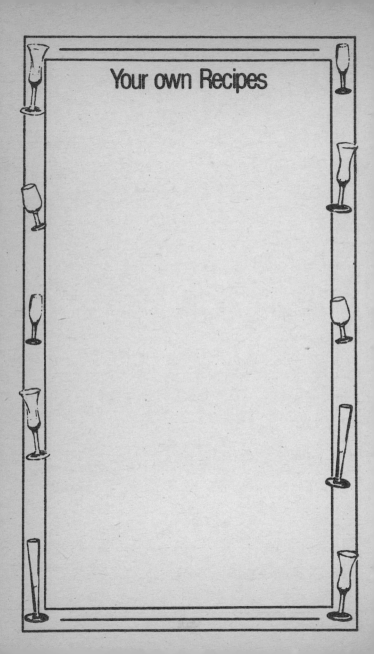

Your own Recipes

C

CAFÉ ROYAL

1½ oz. brandy
Cup of coffee
Whipped cream

Fill coffee cup with hot black coffee. Add the brandy and top with whipped cream.

CAPE CODDER

1½ oz. vodka
3 oz. cranberry juice

Fill a highball glass with ice and add ingredients. (A variation is a Sea Breeze. Substitute grapefruit juice for ½ of the cranberry juice.) No garnish.

CATAWBA COCKTAIL

Nonalcoholic. Pour catawba juice over rocks.

CHAMPAGNE BERRY, Terri's

½ oz. raspberry liqueur (or any berry liqueur)
½ oz. kirsch (cherry liqueur)
4 oz. champagne

Add kirsch and raspberry liqueur to a prechilled champagne glass. Add chilled champagne slowly.

CHAMPAGNE COCKTAIL

Champagne (chilled)
Cube of sugar
Angostura bitters

Dip a sugar cube in Angostura bitters. Drop the sugar cube in a chilled champagne glass. Fill the glass with champagne and mix to dissolve the sugar cube. Garnish with a lemon twist.

CHAMPAGNE PUNCH I

3 bottles of champagne
1 qt. club soda
6 oz. curaçao
3 oz. brandy
3 oz. maraschino
5 oz. lemon juice
8 oz. powdered sugar (superfine)

Combine all except champagne and soda in a punch bowl. Mix well to dissolve the powdered sugar. Then add the champagne and soda along with a block of ice before serving. There are also dry champagne punch mixtures such as Bartenders that make it easy every time. Just add the champagne and ginger ale. To make a block of ice, take the divider out of the ice tray or use an empty milk container cut in half. Block ice dissolves very slowly and should be used.

CHAMPAGNE PUNCH II

1 bottle champagne
½ bottle Southern Comfort
½ liter bottle 7-Up
6 oz. can frozen lemonade
6 oz. can frozen orange juice

Mix all ingredients except the champagne and 7-Up. Add the 7-Up and then the champagne. Include block ice. This is very potent.

CHAMPAGNE SUNSET

1½ oz. orange juice
4 oz. champagne
Dash grenadine

Put orange juice and grenadine in a champagne glass. Add champagne slowly.

CHI CHI

1½ oz. vodka
1 oz. sweetened coconut juice or cream of coconut
3 oz. pineapple juice

Put in a blender for 30 seconds or shake with 1 cup of crushed ice. Pour into a 10 oz. stemmed glass.

CHOCOLATE KISS

1½ oz. crème de cacao
½ oz. cream

Fill a rocks glass with ice. Add ingredients and stir well. No garnish.

CINNAMON KISS

1½ oz. cinnamon schnapps
½ oz. grenadine

Fill a rocks glass with ice. Add ingredients and stir.

CLOVER CLUB

½ oz. lemon juice
1½ oz. gin
3 dashes grenadine
White of 1 egg

Pour ingredients into a shaker with cracked ice. Shake very well. Strain into a large, chilled cocktail glass.

COCONUT DAIQUIRI

1½ oz. rum
3 oz. sweetened lemon juice
Dash lime juice
3 oz. cream of coconut

Pour all ingredients into a blender with 1 cup cracked ice. Blend for 30 seconds and pour into a 10 oz. stemmed glass.

COFFEE COCKTAIL

1 oz. apple brandy
1 oz. port wine
1 egg yolk
Nutmeg

Shake well with ice. Strain and pour into a cocktail glass. Sprinkle with nutmeg.

COFFEE HUMMER

1 oz. coffee liqueur or Kahlúa
1 oz. rum
2 scoops vanilla ice cream

Combine all ingredients in a blender with a scoop of crushed ice. Crushed ice must be used because it keeps the mix thick. Blend for 30 seconds and pour into a 10 oz. stemmed glass.

COFFEE ROYAL

1½ oz. brandy (can use blended whiskey)
1 cup hot black coffee

Add brandy to coffee. You can use sugar at this point to sweeten to taste. This may be garnished with a lemon peel.

COLLINS (Gin, Vodka, Bourbon, Rum, or Brandy Collins)

This is a drink with 1½ oz. of gin, vodka, bourbon, rum, or brandy. The name differs with the liquor used. A sweet-sour mix is used or 1 to 3 oz. of sweetened lemon juice. This is well shaken with ice. Next it is strained into a tall Collins glass and the glass is then filled with club soda.

COLORADO BULLDOG

1 oz. vodka
1 oz. Kahlúa or coffee liqueur
1 oz. cream (half-and-half)
Cola

Fill a hurricane or Collins glass with ice. Pour in the vodka, Kahlúa, then the cream. Fill the glass with cola.

COOLER

Rosé or Burgundy
Sprite

Fill a tall glass with ice. Fill ½ with rosé or Burgundy and fill the rest of the glass with Sprite. Garnish with a lemon wedge.

CUBA LIBRE

1½ oz. rum
Cola

Pour rum over ice in a highball glass. Then fill glass with cola and garnish with a wedge of lime or a dash of lime juice.

(As legend has it, this drink originated at the turn of the century in Cuba. The soldiers were not allowed to drink in uniform. They would ask for a Cuba Libre and the bartender would empty some of the cola from a bottle and add rum. It would be served in a cola bottle with a wedge of lime to disguise the liquor and the odor.)

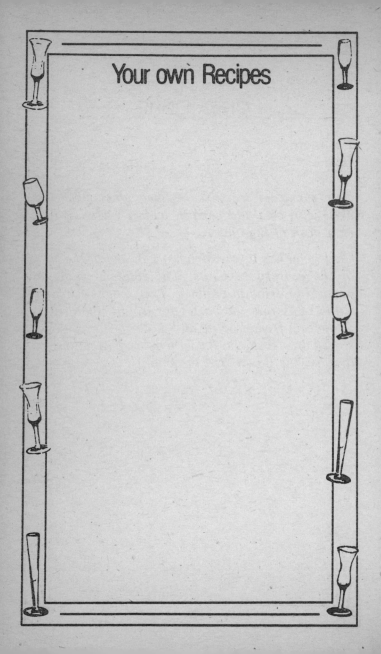

Your own Recipes

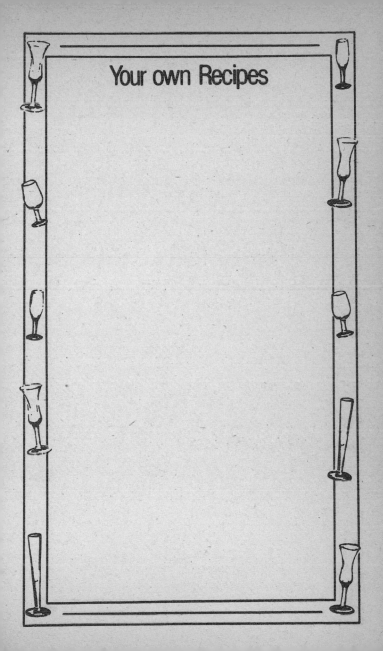

Your own Recipes

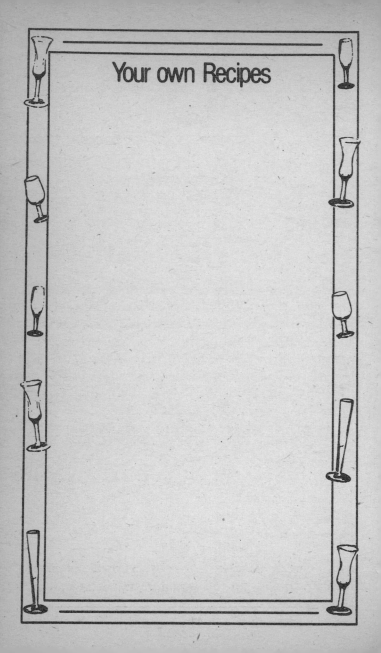

Your own Recipes

D

DAIQUIRI

1½ oz. rum
2 oz. lemon juice or lime juice
½ teaspoon superfine sugar

Put the ingredients in a blender with ice. Blend and pour into a rocks glass or strain into a cocktail glass. This can also be done without a blender by shaking (mixing) the ingredients. (Again, I recommend the use of a sweet-sour mix in place of the lemon and lime juice.) Garnish with a lime wedge.

DAIQUIRI—Banana, Frozen

1½ oz. rum
1½ oz. sweetened lemon juice or lime juice
½ small ripe banana
½ oz. crème de banana (optional)
½ teaspoon superfine sugar

Add ingredients and 1 cup of crushed ice in a blender. Blend for 30 seconds and serve in a chilled stemmed glass. No garnish. (In place of the lemon juice, lime juice, and sugar, you can use a sweet-sour premix.)

DAIQUIRI—Coconut, Frozen

1½ oz. rum
2 oz. sweetened lemon juice or lime juice
3 oz. coconut juice
½ teaspoon superfine sugar

Pour all ingredients into a blender with 1 cup of cracked ice. Blend for 30 seconds and serve in a tall stemmed glass. No garnish. (In place of the lemon juice, lime juice, and sugar, use a sweet-sour premix.)

DAIQUIRI—Peach, Frozen

2 oz. rum
2 oz. sweetened lemon juice or lime juice
½ freshly peeled peach (or canned)
½ teaspoon superfine sugar

Pour all ingredients into a blender with 1 cup of cracked ice. Blend for 30 seconds and serve in a tall stemmed glass. (In place of the lemon juice, lime juice, and sugar, use a sweet-sour premix.)

DAIQUIRI—Raspberry

1½ oz. rum
2 oz. sweetened lemon juice or lime juice
½ cup fresh or frozen raspberries
½ teaspoon superfine sugar

Pour all ingredients into a blender with 1 cup cracked ice. Blend for 30 seconds and pour into a chilled, large stemmed glass. (In place of the lemon juice, lime juice, and sugar, use a sweet-sour premix.)

DAIQUIRI—Strawberry

1½ oz. rum
2 oz. sweetened lemon juice or lime juice
½ cup frozen strawberries or 4 or 5 fresh strawberries
1 teaspoon superfine sugar, if using fresh strawberries

Optional: Cut the strawberries in half and use ½ oz. strawberry liqueur—eliminate sugar if strawberry liqueur is used.

Pour all ingredients into a blender and blend with 1 cup of cracked ice for 30 seconds. Pour into a chilled stemmed glass. Garnish with a fresh, large strawberry if available.

(In place of the lemon juice and lime juice, use a sweet-sour premix.)

DEEP T

½ oz. Baileys Irish Cream
½ oz. vodka
½ oz. Kahlúa

Add ingredients to a shot glass and stir. Rim the outside of a shot glass with whipped cream. The center of the glass is open. Leave the shot glass on the table or bar. It is drunk by bending over and putting the whole shot glass into your mouth. Tilt your head back and drink. (Do not touch the glass with your hands.)

DOLLAR SHOT

Each person in the group takes a dollar bill. The first 3 numbers on each person's dollar become their numbers. Counting from the top left, you use the number and count the bottles until the number is reached. From each of the 3 bottles, ½ oz. is poured into a shot glass. Stir and drink.

DOWN UNDER

1 oz. Irish whiskey
1 oz. Irish cream
1 oz. Kahlúa
2 oz. cream

Chill a brandy snifter and add ice cubes. Pour in ingredients and stir well. No garnish.

DREAMSICLE

1½ oz. Irish cream
4 oz. orange juice

In a chilled rocks glass filled with ice cubes, add ingredients and stir. No garnish.

DRY MANHATTAN

1½ oz. blended whiskey
¼–½ oz. dry vermouth
Dash of Angostura bitters (optional)

To make it straight up, chill a cocktail glass. Fill a shaker with ice and add ingredients. Stir and strain into a cocktail glass. Garnish with an olive, a cherry, or lemon twist.

DRY MARTINI (Robert's favorite)

1½ oz. gin or vodka
Dry vermouth

To make a very dry martini, put two dashes of dry vermouth into a cocktail or rocks glass with nothing else in the glass. Then pour the vermouth out of the glass. Next, if it is on the rocks, fill the glass with ice and add the gin or vodka.

If you want it straight up, then use a chilled cocktail glass, adding the vodka or gin after the vermouth has been poured away. Garnish both the straight-up and on-the-rocks with a lemon twist and an olive. The only way to make a Martini more dry is not to add any vermouth.

DRY ROB ROY

1½ oz. Scotch
¼–½ oz. dry vermouth
Dash of Angostura bitters (Optional)

Follow the same procedure as in the Dry Martini.
Garnish with an olive. To make it extra dry, cut
down on the vermouth or put the vermouth in the
glass and then pour it out before adding the
Scotch.

DUBONNET COCKTAIL

1 oz. Dubonnet (red)
1 oz. gin

Fill a rocks glass with ice and add ingredients. You
can also use a shaker filled with ice and strain into
a cocktail glass. If you want, use a lemon twist as
garnish.

DUTCH COFFEE

1½ oz. chocolate minted liqueur
Hot coffee
Whipped cream

Pour the liqueur into an empty mug. Fill with hot black coffee and top with whipped cream.

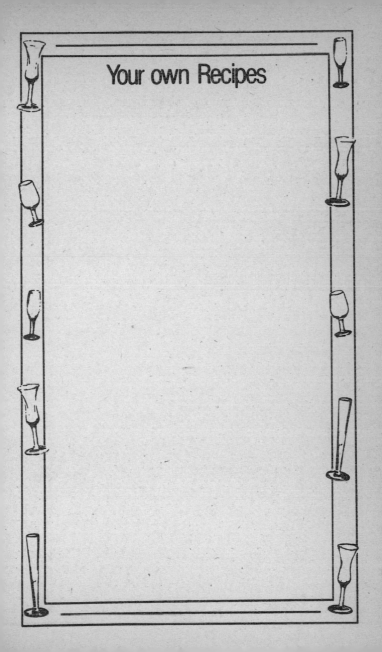

Your own Recipes

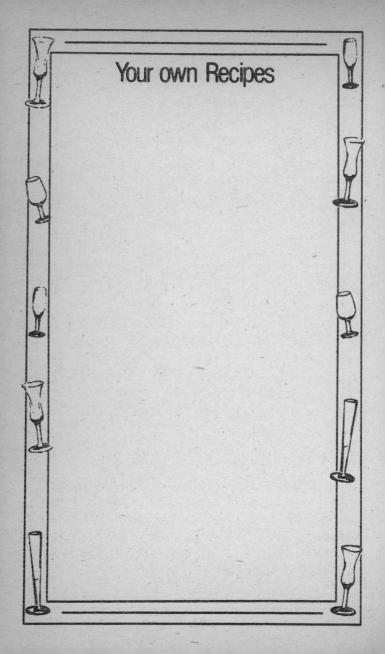

Your own Recipes

E

ED COLLINS

1 oz. anisette
1 oz. schnapps

Serve in a rocks glass over ice. Stir and garnish with a black licorice stick.

EGGNOG—BAHAMIAN, Joni's

1 qt. canned eggnog
12 oz. dark rum
6 oz. Nassau Royale or vanilla liquor
8 oz. whipped cream
Nutmeg

Pour 1 qt. of canned eggnog (or fresh—see Eggnog Brandy) into a punch bowl. Pour in the dark rum and the Nassau Royale. Stir and then fold in the whipped cream. Chill the mixture in your refrigerator. Stir and top each serving with a light dusting of nutmeg. This serves 12.

EGGNOG—BALTIMORE

1 oz. rum
1 oz. brandy
1 oz. Madeira
6 oz. canned dairy eggnog

The basic eggnog recipe is above and can be used in place of the canned eggnog. Combine ingredients with ice and shake vigorously. Strain into a large stemmed or highball glass and top with nutmeg.

EGGNOG—BRANDY OR RUM

2–3 oz. brandy or rum
1 cup milk
1 whole egg
1 teaspoon superfine sugar
2 dashes Angostura bitters

Put ingredients in a shaker with ½ cup crushed ice. Because of the egg, shake hard and long. Strain into a rocks glass and top with nutmeg. It is much easier and more predictable to use a premixed eggnog. Read the premixed dairy eggnog label for variations.

EGGNOG—IRISH

1 qt. canned eggnog
6 oz. dark rum
6 oz. Irish cream
8 oz. whipped cream
Nutmeg

Pour 1 qt. of canned eggnog into a punch bowl. Pour in the rum and the Irish cream. Stir. Fold in one cup (8 oz.) whipped cream. Chill in the refrigerator, stir, and serve. Top each individual serving with nutmeg. Serves 12.

EGGNOG—SOUTHERN COMFORT

1 oz. Southern Comfort
4 oz. canned eggnog

Chill ingredients and stir vigorously together in a rocks glass. Garnish with nutmeg.

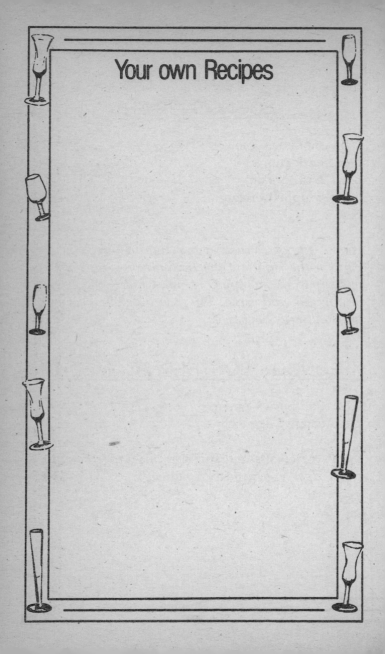

Your own Recipes

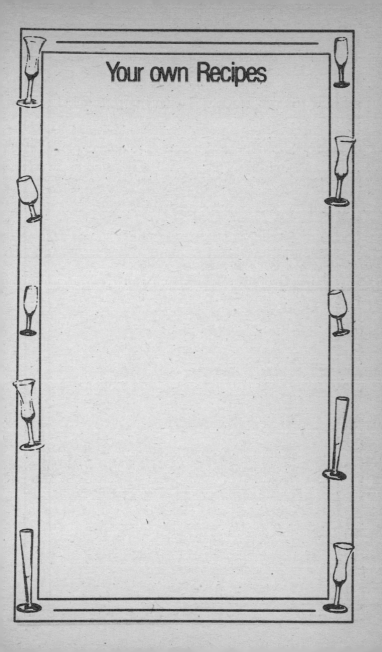

Your own Recipes

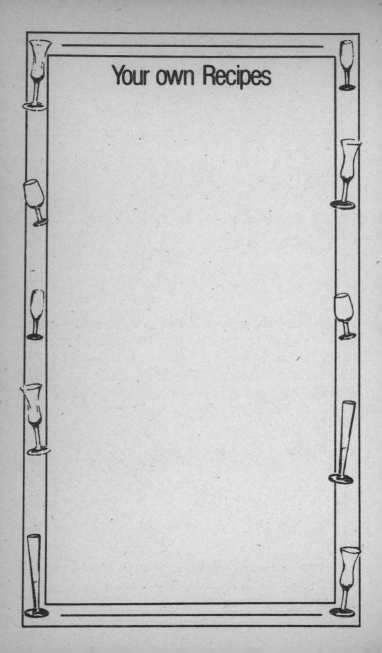

Your own Recipes

F

FIZZ

2 oz. gin (brandy, rum, vodka, or tequila)
½ oz. lemon juice
¼ oz. lime juice
1 tablespoon fine sugar
Club soda or carbonated water

*Combine the liquor you desire and the lemon and
lime juice and sugar. Shake with ice and strain
into a Collins or highball glass with a couple of ice
cubes. Fill with the carbonated water or club
soda. (You can use a sweet-sour premix in place of
the lemon and lime juice and the sugar.)*

FREDDY FUDDPUCKER.

½ oz. tequila
½ oz. Galliano
3 oz. orange juice

*Pour into a shaker. Shake well with cracked ice.
Strain into a Collins glass. The Galliano can also*

be floated on top of the tequila and orange juice by use of an inverted spoon held just inside of glass. (This recipe can be changed to a Harvey Wallbanger, which substitutes vodka for tequila.)

FRENCH CONNECTION

1½ oz. cognac
¾ oz. amaretto

Pour ingredients into a brandy snifter or an ice-filled rocks glass.

FRENCH 75

1½ oz. brandy or gin
1 oz. lemon juice
1 teaspoon fine sugar
Chilled champagne

Take the brandy, lemon juice, and sugar and shake together. Pour into a Collins glass with ice. Then fill the glass with the chilled champagne. (The lemon juice and sugar can be replaced by a sweet-sour premix.) Garnish with an orange and a cherry.

FRITZ'S COFFEE

¾ oz. Frangelico
¾ oz. Irish cream
Coffee

In a coffee mug add ingredients and fill with hot black coffee.

FROZEN DRINKS

To make a frozen drink, use a blender and add a lot of ice and blend longer than recipe suggests. Have more ice than liquid to begin with, but remember that frozen drinks don't have as strong a flavor as unfrozen drinks.

BONUS RECIPE: THE FUZZY NAVEL

1 oz. Peach Schnapps
Orange juice
Ice

Use a 9 or 10 oz. glass and put 1 oz. Peach Schnapps, ice and fill with orange juice.

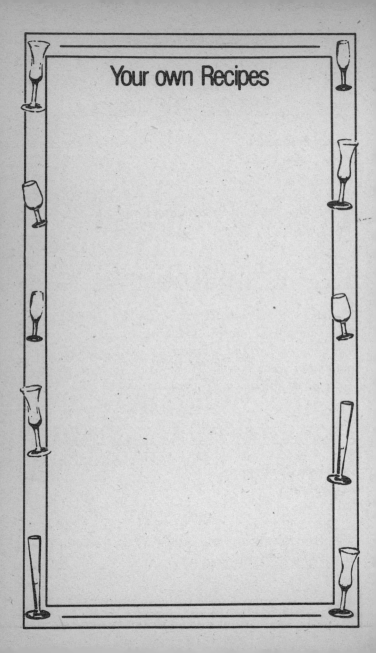

Your own Recipes

Your own Recipes

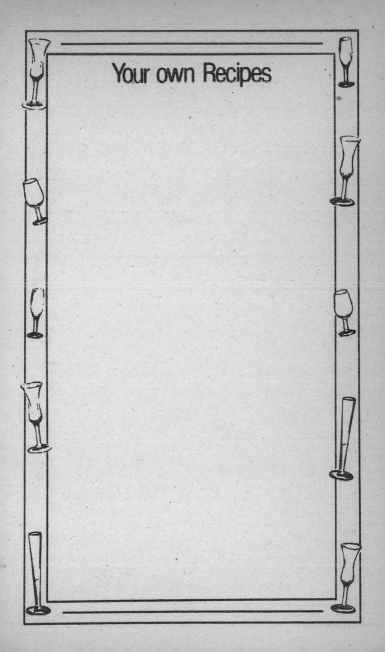

Your own Recipes

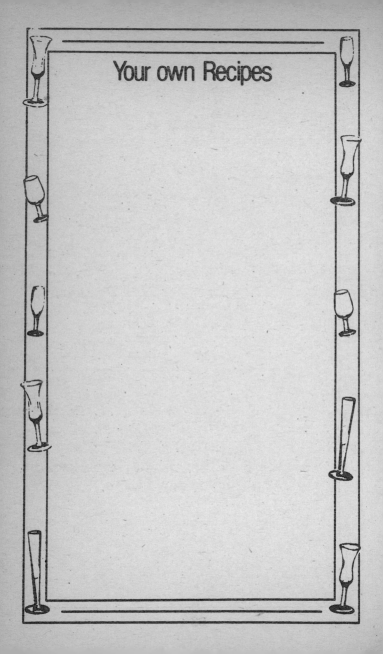

G

GEORGIA PEACH

¾ oz. peach schnapps
¾ oz. Southern Comfort

*Pour ingredients on top of each other. Do not stir.
Do not add ice or chill. This drink is made and
served in a shot glass.*

GIBSON

1½ oz. gin or vodka
Dry vermouth

*See the recipes for Dry Martini and Martini. A
Gibson is a Martini where the olive and/or lemon
peel are exchanged for cocktail onions.*

GIMLET

1¼ oz. gin or vodka
¼ oz. Rose's lime juice

Add ingredients and shake with ice. Strain into a chilled cocktail glass. Garnish with a wedge of lime. (For on the rocks, just use a rocks glass with ice, stir, and garnish with a wedge of lime.)

You can also experiment with rum and tequila and Rose's lime juice.

A tip: If the Rose's turns slightly brownish after a while, it is still good and usable.

(A gimlet is a wood-handled corkscrew.)

GIN BUCK

1½ oz. gin
1 oz. sweetened lime juice
Ginger ale

Fill a rocks glass with ice cubes. Add the gin and lime juice. Then add ginger ale to taste. Stir with the ice cubes gently. Garnish with lime wedge.

GIN FIZZ

1½ oz. gin
¾ oz. sweetened lemon juice
Club soda

Shake the gin and sweetened lemon with cracked ice. The lemon juice should be replaced by a sweet-sour premix. Strain the ingredients into a 10 oz. stemmed glass or Collins glass with ice cubes. Fill with club soda or carbonated water and stir gently with the ice cubes.

GIN AND IT

1½ oz. gin
¾ oz. sweet vermouth

Fill a cocktail shaker with ice and add the gin and sweet vermouth. Stir and strain into an empty chilled cocktail glass. No garnish.

GIN RICKEY

1½ oz. gin
1¼ oz. lime juice
Club soda

Mix the gin and lime juice in a Collins or old-fashioned glass filled with ice cubes. Fill the glass with club soda or carbonated water to taste. Stir gently with the ice cubes. Garnish with a wedge of lime. An alternative recipe is to take the gin at 1½ oz. and squeeze the juice of ½ of a large lime and drop it in the glass and add the club soda.

Alternatives: Substitute brandy, rum, Scotch, sloe gin, whiskey, or vodka for the gin.

GIN SOUR

1½ oz. gin
1 oz. sweetened lemon juice
1 egg white (optional—use for a foamy head)

Use a blender. Blend with ice and pour into a rocks glass or strain into a cocktail glass. Garnish with an orange and cherry. (It is advisable to use a sweet-sour premix to replace the sweetened lemon juice and egg white.)

GIN STONE SOUR

1½ oz. gin
½ oz. orange juice
½ oz. sweetened lemon juice
1 egg white (optional—use for a foamy head)

Use a blender with ice and pour all ingredients into the blender. Blend and strain into a cocktail glass or pour into a rocks glass. Garnish with an orange slice and cherry. (Again, I recommend replacing the lemon juice and egg white with a sweet-sour premix. All ingredients except the gin can be replaced with Collins Stone Sour Mix.)

GIN AND TONIC

1½ oz. gin
Tonic water

Pour gin into an old-fashioned glass with ice cubes. Add tonic water and stir gently, using the ice cubes. Garnish with a lime wedge. For a Vodka and Tonic, just substitute vodka for the gin.

GLOGG
(By Jerome Duke of Lincolnwood)

8 oz. dark raisins
1 oz. pitted prunes
2 whole dried apricots
1–3 inch cinnamon stick
¼ oz. whole cardamom seeds
½ oz. whole cloves
1 piece dried orange peel
3 whole blanched almonds
2 qt. water
1 cup sugar
2 qt. port wine
1 pt. alcohol (190 proof) brandy

Cover fruit-and-spice mixture with water and sugar and boil slowly about 1 hour. Add wine and brandy and bring to a boil again. Remove from heat. May be served hot or cold, with or without fruit. This recipe makes about 22 6 oz. servings.

GODFATHER

1½ oz. Scotch or bourbon
¾ oz. amaretto

Fill a rocks glass with ice cubes and add ingredients. Mix and serve without a garnish.

GODMOTHER

1½ oz. vodka
¾ oz. amaretto

Fill a rocks glass with ice cubes and add ingredients. Mix and serve without a garnish.

GOLDEN CADILLAC

1–1½ oz. Galliano
1 oz. white crème de cacao
1 oz. half-and-half or heavy cream

Shake ingredients with cracked ice or use a blender and strain into a prechilled champagne or cocktail glass. No garnish.

GOLDEN RUSSIAN

¾ oz. vodka
¾ oz. Galliano

Pour ingredients into a shot glass. No ice or garnish.

GOOD AND PLENTY

¾ oz. anisette
¾ oz. blackberry brandy

Shake ingredients with ice, strain, and serve in a shot glass.

GRASSHOPPER

¾ oz. green crème de menthe
¾ oz. white crème de cacao
¾ oz. half-and-half or cream

Blend or shake ingredients with cracked ice. Strain into a champagne or cocktail glass that is prechilled. No garnish is used here.

GREEN LIZARD

1 oz. green Chartreuse
¼ oz. Bacardi "151" rum

Served in a shot glass. Pour in the green Chartreuse and float the "151" rum. A very potent drink. Legend has it that this was originated at a bowling machine in P.O.E.T.S. establishment. The loser has to drink what the winner calls. The victor chooses this, as the loser will be unable to see the pins in the next game.

GREYHOUND

1½ oz. vodka
Grapefruit juice

Using a highball glass filled with ice, add the vodka. Next pour grapefruit juice to fill the glass. Stir well. The amount of grapefruit juice can be varied by the size of the glass and the amount of ice. No garnish.

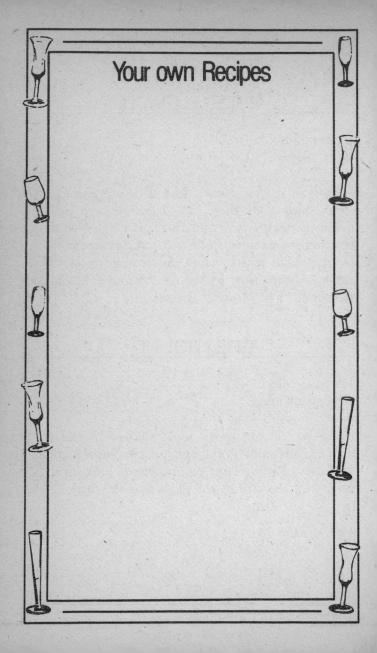

Your own Recipes

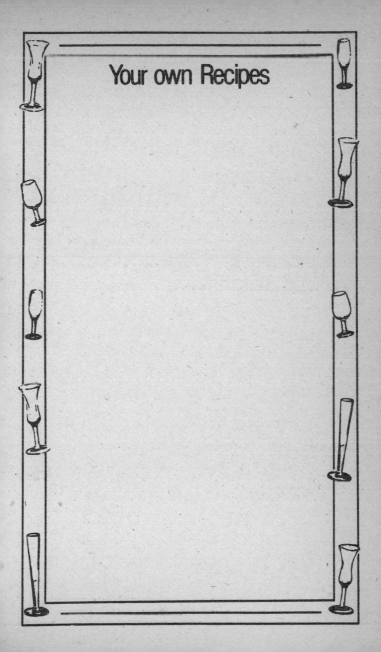

Your own Recipes

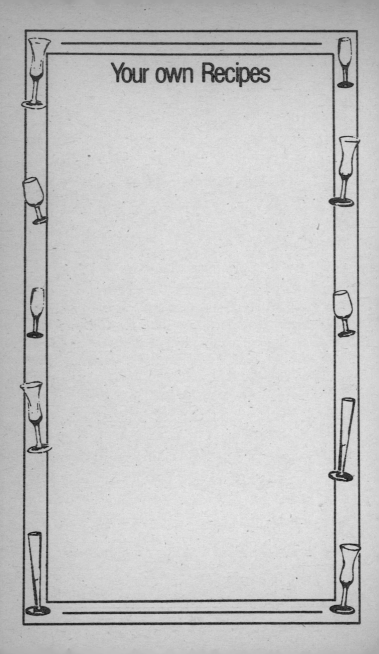

Your own Recipes

H

HARVEY WALLBANGER

1½ oz. vodka
¾ oz. Galliano
Orange juice

Pour the vodka into a tall glass (a Collins glass) filled with ice. Next, fill the glass almost to the top with orange juice. Then top with the Galliano. To float the Galliano, invert a spoon and hold it inside the glass with the top just touching the inside wall. Pour the Galliano slowly onto the spoon. No garnish is used.

HEART ATTACK

1 oz. cinnamon schnapps
½ oz. Malort
½ oz. grenadine

Serve in a rocks glass with ice cubes and stir.

HEARTBURNS

1½ oz. cinnamon schnapps
½ oz. Tabasco sauce

Fill a rocks glass with ice, add ingredients, and stir.

HOT APPLE PIE

1½ oz. Rock & Rye
Apple cider
¼ teaspoon cinnamon
¼ teaspoon nutmeg
¼ teaspoon cloves (powdered)

Season apple cider to taste with spices. Heat. Pour Rock & Rye into a coffee mug, then add hot cider and top with whipped cream. If this drink is properly made, it really tastes like apple pie!

HOT APPLE TODDY

1½ oz. apple brandy
Hot apple cider

Pour the apple brandy in a coffee mug. Then add heated apple cider to fill the mug. Garnish with a cinnamon stick.

HOT BUTTERED RUM

1 large teaspoon Hot Butter Rum (premix).
1½ oz. rum

Put rum batter and rum into a coffee mug. Fill with hot water and stir well. Garnish with a cinnamon stick.

To make a batch of your own scratch batter, do the following:

2 lb. unsalted butter
2 lb. brown sugar
1 teaspoon cinnamon
4 oz. cream or half-and-half

Melt the butter in a saucepan and add the brown sugar and cinnamon. Keep stirring on a low fire until smooth. Then add the cream and turn the fire off. This mixture can be stored in the refrigerator. When ready to serve, use 1 tablespoon of the mix with 1½ oz. of rum. Then add hot water to the ingredients already in the coffee mug. Stir well and garnish with a cinnamon stick. You can also top with nutmeg.

HOT TODDY

1½ oz. brandy or whiskey
Hot tea or plain hot water
1 teaspoon sugar

Pour the brandy or whiskey into a coffee mug. Then fill with hot tea or hot water and add a teaspoon of sugar. Stir and garnish with a lemon twist or nutmeg.

HUMMER

1 oz. coffee liqueur (or Kahlúa)
1 oz. rum
2 scoops vanilla ice cream

Combine all ingredients in a blender with a scoop of crushed ice. Crushed ice is used because it keeps the mixture thick. Blend for 30 seconds and pour into a large stemmed glass.

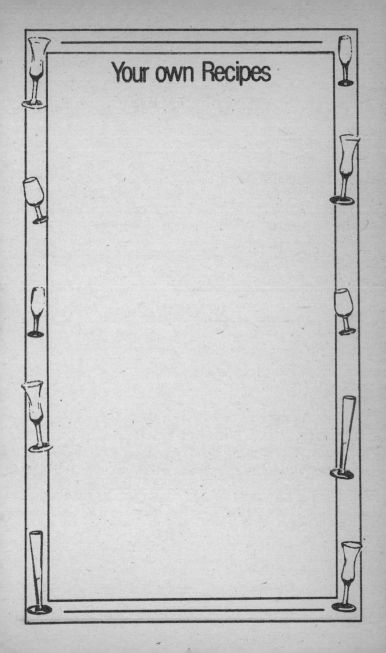

Your own Recipes

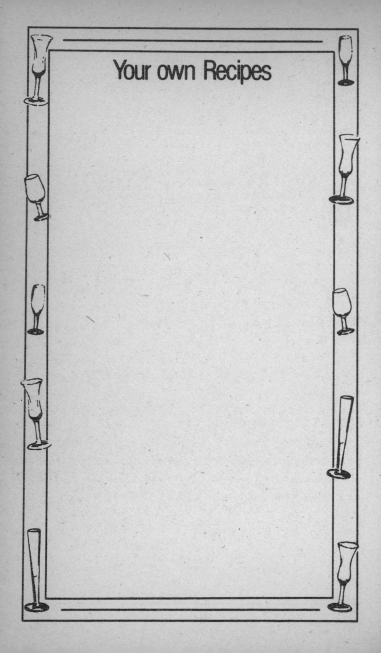

Your own Recipes

I

ICED TEA—LONG ISLAND

½ oz. gin
½ oz. vodka
½ oz. rum
½ oz. tequila
¼ oz. Triple Sec
1½ oz. sweetened lemon juice
Dash of lime juice
Cola

Fill a Collins glass or a large tumbler with ice. Add all the ingredients except the cola. Stir the ingredients and add cola until the drink becomes the color of tea. (Again, I suggest replacing the lemon and lime juice with a sweet-sour premix. If Collins Long Island Iced Tea is in your store, try it. It tastes like iced tea and you only need add vodka and the cola.) Garnish with a lemon wedge or twist.

IRISH COFFEE

1½ oz. Irish whiskey
¼ oz. Kahlúa
Coffee
Whipped cream
Crème de menthe (green)

First, put whiskey and Kahlúa in a coffee mug. Next add hot black coffee. Top with whipped cream. Pour a small amount of green crème de menthe over the whipped cream. The Kahlúa is used in place of sugar.

IRISH COFFEE—(Variation)

1½ oz. Irish whiskey
1 teaspoon brown sugar
Coffee
Whipped cream

In a coffee mug pour the whiskey and brown sugar. Next pour in hot black coffee. Top with whipped cream.

IRISH COFFEE—OLD STANDARD

1½ oz. Irish whiskey
Hot black coffee
1 teaspoon superfine sugar
Dash green crème de menthe
Whipped cream

Pour Irish whiskey into a coffee cup. Fill with coffee, add sugar, and top with whipped cream. Pour a dash of green crème de menthe over the whipped cream.

IRISH DELIGHT

¾ oz. Irish cream
¾ oz. Irish whiskey

Fill a rocks glass with ice. Pour ingredients over the ice and stir. No garnish.

ITALIAN COFFEE

1½ oz. amaretto
Coffee
Whipped cream

Pour the amaretto in a coffee mug. Next add hot black coffee and stir. Top with whipped cream.

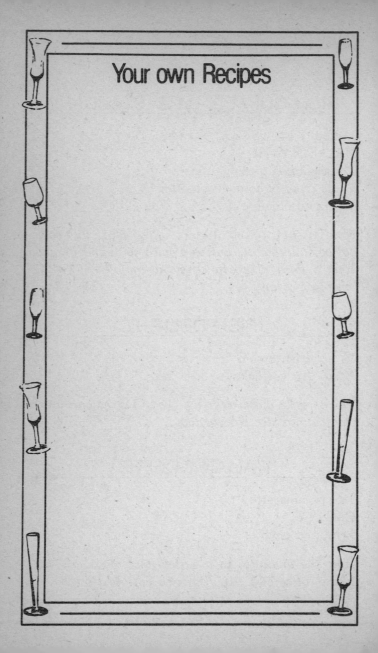

Your own Recipes

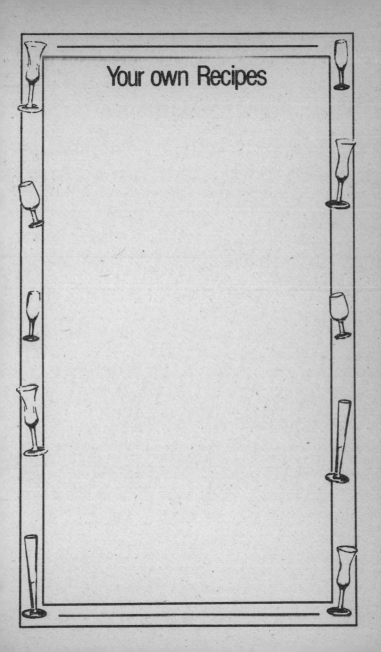

Your own Recipes

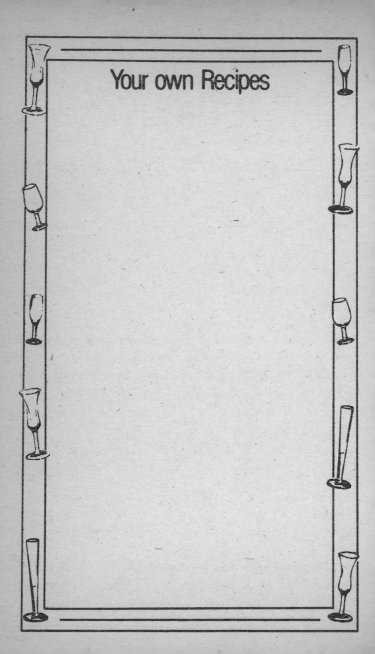

Your own Recipes

J

JACK ROSE

1 oz. applejack
⅓ oz. grenadine
1 oz. lime juice
Dash of Lemon juice

Add ingredients to a shaker. Shake well with ice and strain into a prechilled cocktail glass. (Again, I recommend substituting a sweet-sour premix for the lemon and lime juice.)

JAMAICAN COFFEE

1½ oz. rum
½ oz. Kahlúa or Tia Maria
Coffee
Whipped cream

In a coffee mug add rum and Kahlúa. Then fill with hot black coffee. Top with whipped cream.

JELLY BEAN

½ oz. anisette
½ oz. blackberry brandy

In a small brandy snifter or cocktail or shot glass, pour in anisette and float brandy on top. To float the brandy, invert a spoon and pour the brandy gently over the spoon into the glass.

This drink can also be made by pouring over ice cubes in a rocks glass. No garnish is used here.

JOHN COLLINS

1½ oz. whiskey
¾ oz. lemon juice
Club soda

Mix the whiskey and lemon juice together with ice. Shake well and strain into a Collins glass with ice cubes. This mixture should be ⅘ full in the Collins glass. Then top with club soda and stir very gently. Garnish with an orange slice and a cherry. You should also serve with a short straw. (Again, a sweet-sour premix should be used in place of the lemon juice.)

Your own Recipes

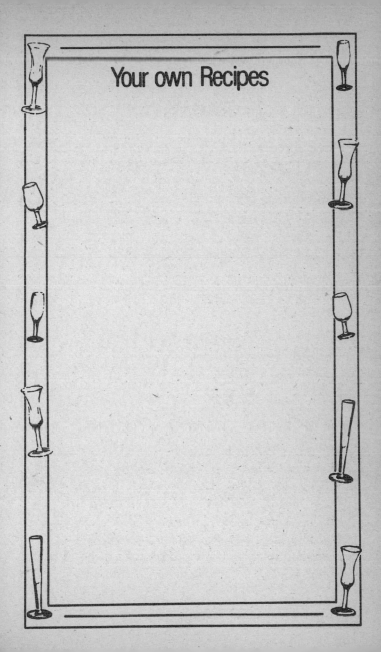

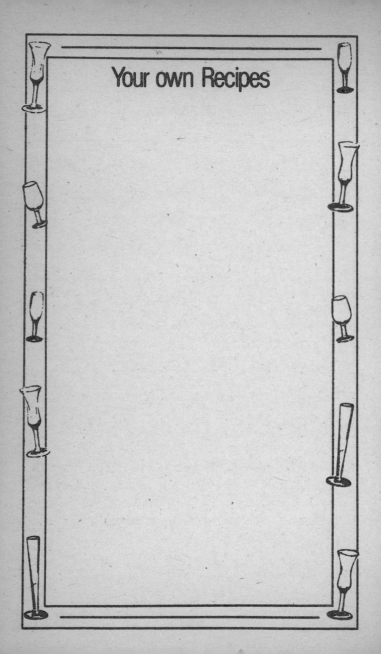

Your own Recipes

K

KAHLÚA AND CREAM

1½ oz. Kahlúa
¾ oz. cream or half-and-half

Pour the Kahlúa into an ice-filled rocks glass or an empty pony or cordial glass. Float cream on top. No garnish.

KAHLÚA HUMMER

1 oz. Kahlúa
1 oz. rum
2 scoops vanilla ice cream

Combine all ingredients in a blender with a scoop of crushed ice. It is important to use crushed ice because it will keep the mix thick. Blend for 30 seconds and pour into a large stemmed glass.

KAMIKAZE

1 oz. vodka
Splash (½ oz.) Rose's lime juice
Splash (½ oz.) Triple Sec or Cointreau

Fill a cocktail shaker with ice. Add the ingredients, stir, and strain into a shot glass or into an ice-filled rocks glass. (An excellent premix, "Collins Kamikaze," is available. It will save you money, and the results are uniformly good.)

This is smoother than a gimlet but is sometimes referred to as a mini-gimlet when served in a shot glass.

KEOKE COFFEE I
(pronounced, Kee-oh-kee)

¾ oz. rum
¾ oz. brandy
¾ oz. Kahlúa
Whipped cream
Coffee

Pour the rum, brandy, and Kahlúa into a coffee mug. Mix with hot black coffee and top with whipped cream. This drink is so popular there is a second recipe following. Try them both and choose which you like better.

KEOKE COFFEE II (Jean's favorite)

½ oz. dark crème de cacao
½ oz. brandy
½ oz Kahlúa or coffee liqueur
Hot coffee
Whipped cream

Pour the crème de cacao, brandy, and Kahlúa into a coffee mug. Fill the mug with hot coffee and top with whipped cream.

KIDDIE COOLER

6 oz. ginger ale
½ oz. Collins Cherry Juice

Serve in a Collins glass with ice cubes. Garnish with a slice of orange and a cherry.

KIDDIE COCKTAIL

6 oz. club soda
1 oz. grenadine

Fill a Collins glass with ice cubes. Add ingredients and stir gently. Garnish with a cherry.

KING ALFONSO

1½ oz. dark crème de cacao
¾ oz. sweet cream

Using a large cordial glass, pour in the crème de cacao. Float the sweet cream on top. No garnish.

KIR (pronounced, Keer)

White wine (Chablis)
½ teaspoon crème de cassis

Prechill a wineglass. Fill with a chilled white wine. Add cassis to make wine a deep rose color. The more cassis added, the sweeter the taste. Stir gently. Garnish with a lemon twist.

KIR ROYAL

Champagne
½ teaspoon crème de cassis or raspberry liqueur

Using a prechilled champagne glass, fill it with chilled champagne and add the cassis or raspberry liqueur. Stir gently. No garnish.

KOOL-AID

¾ oz. vodka or Southern Comfort
¾ oz. amaretto
1 oz. cranberry juice

To make by the shot, fill a cocktail shaker with ice and add all 3 ingredients. Stir and strain into a shot glass.

To make in a highball glass, start by filling the highball glass with ice. Add the vodka and amaretto. Stir gently and fill the glass with cranberry juice. Use more cranberry juice here than you would for a shot. No garnish is used in this drink.

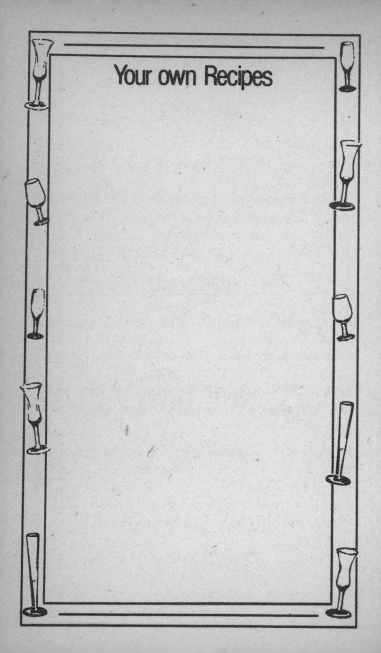

Your own Recipes

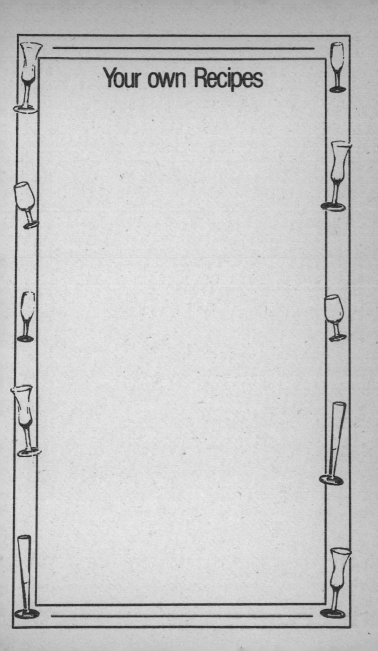

Your own Recipes

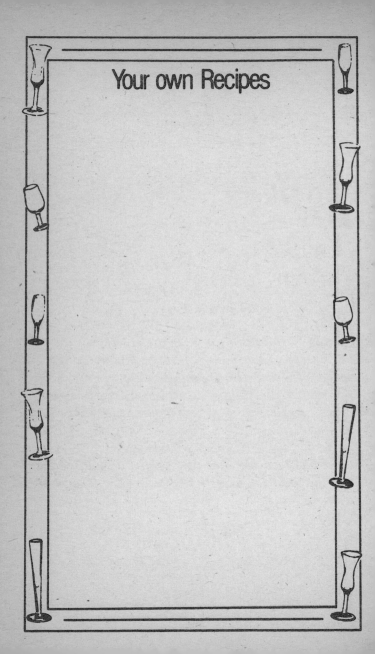

Your own Recipes

L

LONG ISLAND ICED TEA

½ oz. gin
½ oz. vodka
½ oz. rum
½ oz. tequila
½ oz. Triple Sec
1½ oz. sweetened lemon juice
Cola

Fill a Collins glass or a large tumbler with ice. Add all the ingredients except the cola. Stir the ingredients and add cola until the drink becomes the color of iced tea. (Again, I suggest replacing the lemon juice with a sweet-sour premix. If Collins Long Island Iced Tea is in your store, try it. It tastes like iced tea and you only need add vodka and the cola.) Garnish with a lemon wedge or twist.

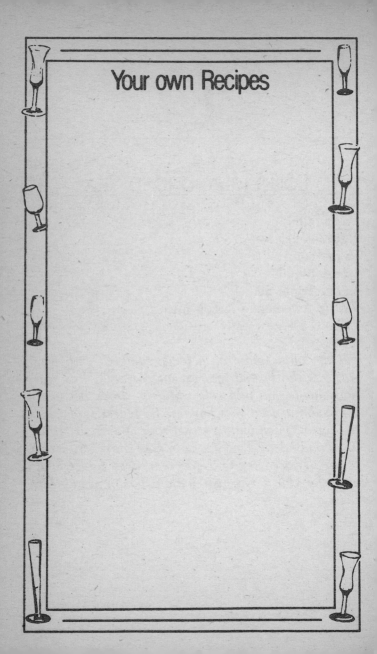

Your own Recipes

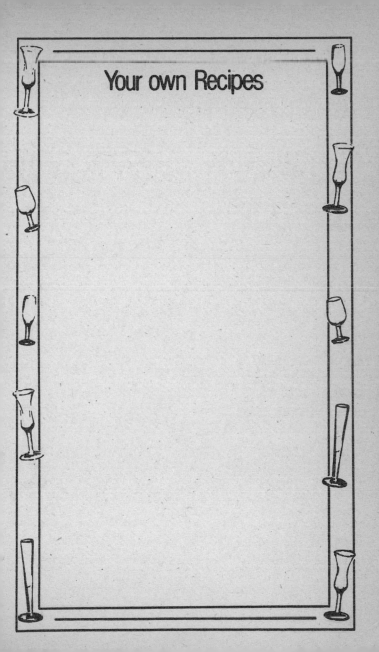

Your own Recipes

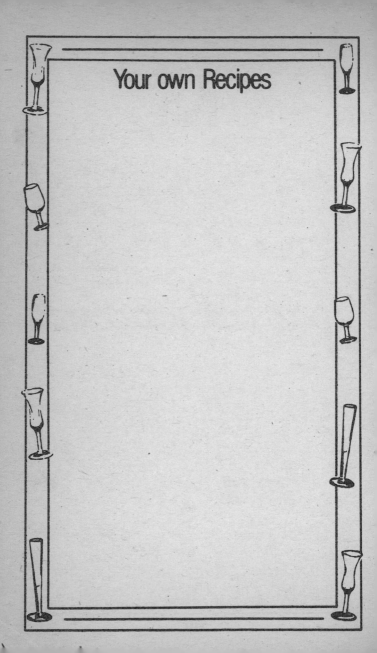

Your own Recipes

M

MAI TAI I

1½ oz. light rum
½ oz. dark rum
Dash of grenadine
3 oz. pineapple juice

Shake ingredients with 1 cup cracked ice and pour into a large stemmed glass and garnish with a pineapple wedge and cherry.

MAI TAI II

½ oz. apricot brandy
½ oz. orange curaçao
½ oz. dark rum
1 oz. pineapple juice
¼ oz. cherry brandy

Shake all ingredients, except cherry brandy, with cracked ice. Strain into a highball glass with crushed ice. As a topping, float ¼ oz. of cherry brandy. Garnish with a pineapple wedge.

MAI TAI III

1 oz. light rum
½ oz. dark rum
½ dash grenadine
¼ oz. orgeat or almond syrup
¼ oz. curaçao or Triple Sec

Combine ingredients in a shaker with cracked ice. Strain into a large stemmed glass or old-fashioned glass. The prechilled glass should be half filled with cracked ice. Use a pineapple stick and a cherry for garnish. Also, provide short straw for sipping.

MAMIE TAYLOR

2 oz. Scotch
½ oz. lime juice
Ginger ale

Fill a highball glass with ice cubes. Next, add the Scotch and lime juice. Stir and add ginger ale to fill. Garnish with a lemon twist.

MANHATTAN

1½ oz. whiskey
¼–½ oz. sweet vermouth
Dash of Angostura bitters (optional)

In a rocks glass filled with ice, add vermouth first, as it is lighter than whiskey and will float to the top if added after the whiskey. Stir and garnish with a cherry.

To make it straight up, chill a cocktail glass. Fill a shaker with ice and add ingredients. Stir and strain into the cocktail glass and garnish with a cherry. (To make a Rob Roy, substitute Scotch for whiskey in this recipe.)

MANHATTAN—BRANDY

1½ oz. brandy
½ oz. sweet vermouth
Dash of Angostura bitters (optional)

Use a brandy snifter and fill it with ice. Add the vermouth first, then the brandy and Angostura. Stir firmly. Garnish with a cherry.

To make it straight up, chill the brandy snifter or stemmed glass. Fill a shaker with ice and add ingredients. Stir and strain into glass.

MANHATTAN—DRY

1½ oz. whiskey
½ oz. dry vermouth
Dash of Angostura bitters (optional)

Using a rocks glass filled with ice, add the dry vermouth first. Then add the whiskey and, if you desire, the Angostura. Stir. Garnish with a lemon twist or olive.

To make straight up, chill a large stemmed glass or snifter. Fill a shaker with ice and add the ingredients. Stir and strain into the glass. To make a Southern Comfort Manhattan, use Southern Comfort instead of whiskey in the Dry Manhattan recipe.

MANHATTAN—PERFECT

1½ oz. whiskey
¼ oz. sweet vermouth
¼ oz. dry vermouth

Put the vermouth, both dry and sweet, in an ice-filled old-fashioned glass. Next pour in the whiskey and strain. Garnish with a lemon twist or a cherry. To make it straight up, put the ingredi-

ents into an ice-filled shaker. Stir and strain into a prechilled cocktail glass.

(A Perfect Rob Roy is made by substituting Scotch for whiskey.)

MANHATTAN—WISCONSIN

2 oz. blended whiskey
¾ oz. sweet vermouth
¼ oz. Collins Cherry Juice

Pour into a shaker and stir with ice. Strain into a prechilled cocktail glass. Garnish with a cherry. This mix can also be served in an old-fashioned glass with ice.

MARGARITA (Karen's Favorite)

1½ oz. tequila
½ oz. Triple Sec
½ oz. lime juice, unsweetened

Begin by wetting the rim of the cocktail glass with a fresh lime or lime juice. The easiest way is to invert the glass and dip it into lime juice. Next, while the rim is still wet, dip it into a plate of salt *so that the glass is rimmed with salt. (You can also use Collins Margarita Salt in a container.)*

Put the tequila, Triple Sec, and unsweetened lime juice into a blender. Mix. Add ice and pour into a cocktail glass. If you want the drink straight up, merely strain from blender. (This recipe can also be done with a sweet-sour premix in place of the lime juice. Cointreau can be used in place of Triple Sec. In place of the unsweetened lime juice, you can also experiment with Rose's lime juice.) Garnish with a slice of lime. This is a recipe that you should experiment with to see which you prefer.

To make a Strawberry Margarita, add two fresh or frozen strawberries and ½ oz. of strawberry liqueur.

To make a Super Margarita, use 1½ oz. tequila, 1½ oz. Cointreau, and ½ oz. fresh lime juice and follow the other directions above in making.

To make a Banana Margarita, add ½ of a ripe banana and ½ oz. of banana liqueur to the above recipe.

MARTINI—(Standard)

1½ oz. gin or vodka
½ oz. dry vermouth

To make it on the rocks, fill a rocks glass with ice and add the vermouth and gin or vodka. Stir gently and garnish with an olive and/or a lemon twist.

If the Martini is straight up, then prechill a cocktail glass. Fill a cocktail shaker with ice, add ingredients, stir, and strain into a cocktail glass. Garnish with an olive and/or a lemon twist.

MARTINI—EXTRA DRY

1½ oz. gin or vodka
Dry vermouth

To make a very dry Martini, put two dashes of dry vermouth into a cocktail or rocks glass with nothing else in the glass. Then pour the vermouth out of the glass. Next, if it is on the rocks, fill the glass with ice and add the gin or vodka.

If you want it straight up, use a chilled cocktail glass and add the vodka or gin to it after the vermouth has been poured away. Garnish both the straight-up and on-the-rocks with a lemon twist and/or an olive. The only way to make a Martini any more dry is not to add any vermouth.

You may also pour the vermouth into the ice and then strain the ice out. This will also make a very dry Martini.

The super-dry Martini is made by filling a glass with ice cubes and pouring in 1½ oz. of gin or vodka. Then the vermouth bottle is lifted into the air and replaced in the same spot without pouring. Garnish with lemon twist and/or olive.

VARIATIONS

Gin Gibson—Substitute cocktail onions for olives and use gin.

Vodka Gibson—Substitute onions for olives and use vodka.

Silver Bullet—Substitute Scotch for the vermouth and use gin.

Vodka Silver Bullet—Substitute vodka for gin and Scotch for vermouth.

Silver Bullets have no garnish.

Slippery Knob—Substitute Grand Marnier for vermouth.

MARTINI, Tom Carney's

1½ oz. gin
Dash dry vermouth
½ teaspoon olive juice (not oil)

Fill an old-fashioned glass with ice. Add the gin and a dash of vermouth. Now, from the jar of olives add ½ teaspoon of olive juice. Stir well and garnish with a queen olive.

MARTINI, Scotty's

1½ oz. gin
¼ oz. dry vermouth
Dash of orange bitters or
    2 dashes of Angostura bitters

Using a mix glass with large ice cubes, pour in ingredients and hand stir. Strain into a cocktail glass and garnish with a twist of lemon and/or an olive.

MARTINI—Rum or Tequila

Merely substitute a good rum or tequila for the gin or vodka in the same proportions as the standard recipe.

MARTINI—Sweet

Substitute sweet vermouth for dry vermouth and use in the same proportions as the standard recipe.

(Also you can try Collins Lemon Twist Mist, which is a lemon spray in a tube. It is excellent for Martinis.)

MARY PICKFORD

1½ oz. light rum
¾ oz. pineapple juice
Dash grenadine

Fill a mixing glass halfway with shaved ice. Next add ingredients and shake. Strain into a prechilled cocktail glass and garnish with a lemon twist.

MELON BALL

1 oz. Midori melon liqueur
½ oz. vodka
2 oz. orange juice (or substitute pineapple or
  grapefruit juice)

*Combine ingredients in a cocktail shaker with ice.
Shake well and strain into a small snifter.*

*You can also double all the ingredients and strain
into a Collins glass with ice. Garnish with an
orange slice, pineapple stick, or cherry.*

MEXICAN COFFEE I

1½ oz. Tia Maria
Coffee
Whipped cream

*Pour Tia Maria into a coffee cup. Add hot black
coffee almost to the top of the cup. Stir and top
with whipped cream.*

MEXICAN COFFEE II

1½ oz. Kahlúa
Coffee
Whipped cream

Pour the Kahlúa into a coffee mug. Add hot black coffee almost to the top. Stir and then add whipped cream.

MIDORI SOUR

1½ oz. Midori melon liqueur
3 oz. lemon juice

Blend or shake with 1 cup of cracked ice. Pour into an old-fashioned glass or strain into a prechilled stemmed glass. (The lemon juice should be replaced with a sweet-sour premix. A premix should also contain a foamy-head ingredient.)

MIDORI STONE SOUR

1½ oz. Midori melon liqueur
1½ oz. lemon juice
1½ oz. orange juice

Blend or shake with 1 cup of cracked ice. Pour into an old-fashioned glass or strain into a prechilled stemmed glass. (The lemon juice should be replaced by a sweet-sour premix and all ingredients except the Midori should be replaced by Collins Stone Sour Mix. Any premix should contain a foamy-head ingredient.)

MIMOSA—STANDARD

Champagne
Orange juice

Using a large tulip or champagne glass, fill it ½ with chilled orange juice and fill the other half with chilled champagne. Stir.

MIMOSA—(Special and Better)

1½ oz. orange juice
½ oz. Triple Sec
Champagne
½ oz. sweet-sour premix (optional)

Blend orange juice and Triple Sec (sweet-sour premix optional) with ice to a frozen consistency. Pour into a champagne glass and fill with champagne. Stir to mix and serve. This is convenient for a party, as you can make in large batches.

MINT JULEP

3 oz. bourbon
3 sprigs of mint
1 teaspoon superfine sugar
1 tablespoon water

Take the water, mint, and sugar and muddle (mash) until the mint is easily smelled. Put these ingredients into a Collins or large stemmed glass. Fill with shaved ice and add bourbon. Stir until prechilled glass is frosted. Garnish with a slice of orange and float some mint sprigs on top.

MINTED MOCHA

1½ oz. peppermint schnapps
Hot chocolate
Whipped cream

Using a coffee mug, put in the peppermint schnapps. Add your own recipe for hot chocolate or use an instant hot chocolate mix, as do most bars. Make sure it is very hot. Stir ingredients and top with whipped cream. This is very good and popular.

ALMOND MOCHA substitutes

Amaretto—for schnapps
Banana Mocha—substitute Banana liqueur for
   schnapps
Mist—means crushed ice
Scotch Mist—means Scotch with shaved or crushed
ice and nothing more.

MOM'S APPLE PIE

1½ oz. apple schnapps
½ oz. cinnamon schnapps

Pour the apple schnapps in a shot glass. Float the cinnamon schnapps on top. (It can also be made in a rocks glass. Fill with ice and add the apple schnapps. Float the cinnamon schnapps on top.)

MOSCOW MULE

1½ oz. vodka
½ fresh lime juice
Ginger beer

Use, if possible, a copper mug called a mule mug. Otherwise use a highball glass. Add the vodka and juice from ½ of a fresh lime. Pour over ice and fill with ginger beer. Garnish with a lime wedge.

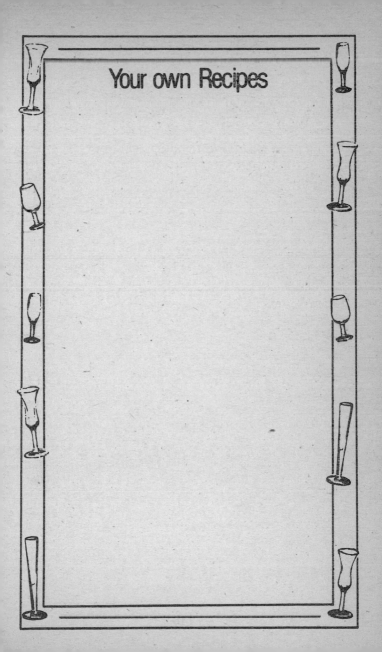

Your own Recipes

Your own Recipes

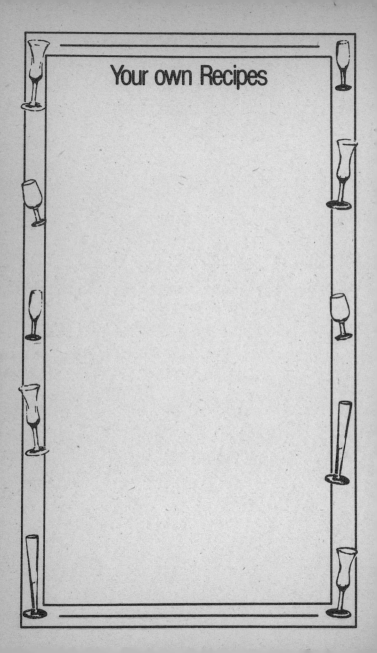

N

NEGRONI

¾ oz. Campari
¾ oz. gin
¾ oz. sweet vermouth

Fill a rocks glass with ice and add ingredients. Stir and garnish with a lemon twist.

To serve straight up, mix ingredients in a shaker and strain into a prechilled stemmed glass.

Your own Recipes

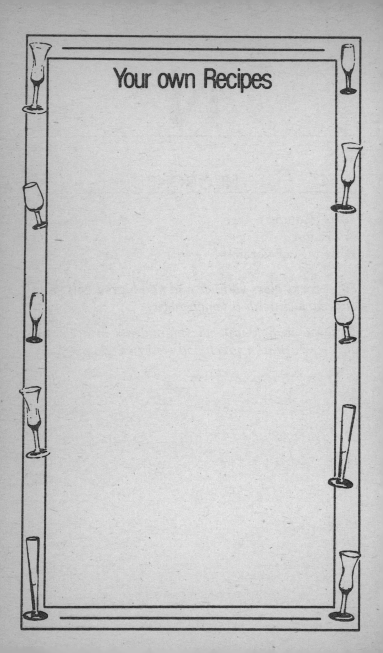

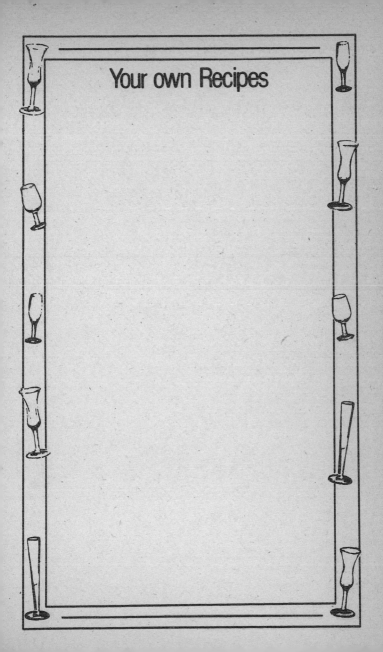

Your own Recipes

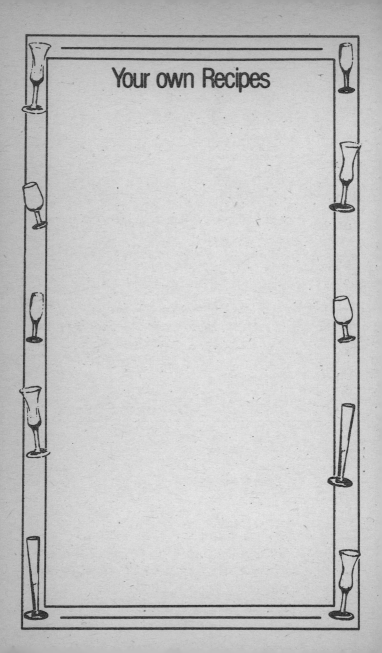

Your own Recipes

O

OLD FASHIONED—STANDARD

1¾ oz. whiskey
1 teaspoon superfine sugar
½ teaspoon Angostura bitters
Club soda

In an empty rocks glass, combine sugar, bitters, and whiskey. Stir to blend. Add ice and fill glass with soda. Add an orange slice and cherry. You can substitute cherry juice for the sugar.

OLD FASHIONED, Tom Carney's

6 dashes Angostura bitters
¾ oz. bar syrup
1½ oz. blended whiskey
Club soda

Fill a 15 oz. old-fashioned glass with ice. Add bitters, bar syrup, and whiskey. Mix well and add the club soda and stir. Garnish with an olive and cinnamon stick.

For a sweeter Old Fashioned, you can use Sprite or cherry juice instead of club soda.

The blended whiskey can be substituted with bourbon, brandy, Southern Comfort, or Scotch. Also, the soda can be cut down according to your taste, or you can use 7-Up or water instead of Sprite or club soda.

OLD FASHIONED—Wisconsin

1½ oz. brandy
1 teaspoon superfine sugar
¼ oz. Collins Cherry Juice
3 dashes Angostura bitters
Club soda

Mix the sugar and cherry juice in an old-fashioned glass filled with ice. Add the bitters and the brandy. Top with a splash of club soda. Garnish with a cherry.

ORANGE BLOSSOM

1½ oz. gin
½ orange
1 teaspoon sugar

Fill a mixing glass ½ full with cracked ice. Add the juice from ½ fresh orange (or 2 oz. of orange juice) and muddle (crush) the sugar. Add the gin and shake well. Strain into a prechilled cocktail glass and garnish with a slice of orange.

ORGASM

¾ oz. vodka
¾ oz. Kahlúa or coffee liqueur (optional)
¾ oz. Bailey's or Irish Cream

Blend ingredients with ice and pour into a rocks glass. To make it straight up, just strain after blending and pour into a prechilled cocktail or stemmed glass. No garnish.

Variation   *Screaming Orgasm*

¾ oz. vodka
¾ oz. Bailey's or Irish Cream
¾ oz. Kahlúa (optional) or coffee liqueur
¾ oz. amaretto

Blend ingredients with ice and pour into a rocks glass. For a straight-up, strain into a prechilled stemmed glass. No garnish.

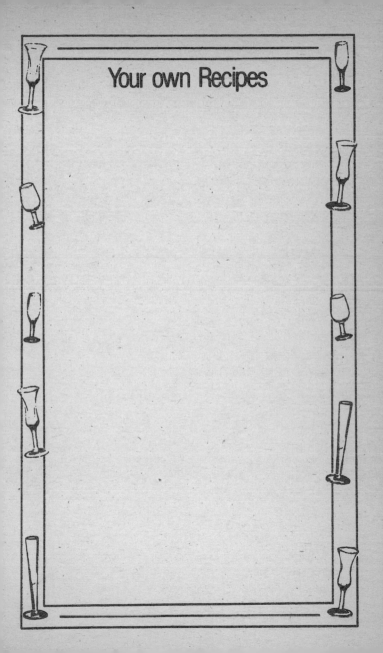

Your own Recipes

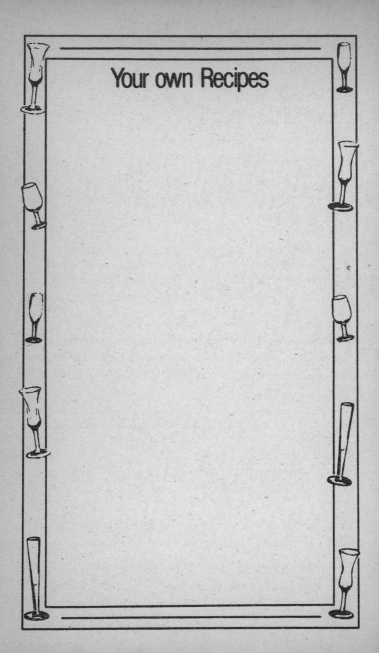

Your own Recipes

P

PERFECT MANHATTAN

1½ oz. whiskey
¼ oz. sweet vermouth
¼ oz. dry vermouth

Put the vermouth in an ice-filled old-fashioned glass. Then add the whiskey. Stir well and garnish with a lemon twist.

To make it straight up, use a shaker and add ingredients with cracked ice. Shake well and strain into a prechilled cocktail glass.

PERFECT ROB ROY

1½ oz. Scotch
¼ oz. sweet vermouth
¼ oz. dry vermouth

Put the two vermouths in an ice-filled old-fashioned glass. Then add the Scotch and stir well.

To make it straight up, use a shaker with ice and mix and strain into a prechilled cocktail glass.

PERNOD

1½ oz. Pernod

Put the Pernod in a highball glass with a couple of ice cubes. Fill the glass with water or add water to your own taste.

PIMM'S CUP

1½ oz. Pimm's No. 1 Cup
1 oz. gin
Club soda

Fill a rocks glass with ice and add the Pimm's and gin. Fill the glass with club soda and garnish with a cucumber slice.

PIÑA COLADA

1½ oz. rum
2 oz. unsweetened pineapple juice
1 oz. cream of coconut

In a blender combine all ingredients with crushed ice. Blend for 30 seconds or until mixture is smooth.

Serve as soon as you take it out of the blender. Garnish with a pineapple wedge.

The Piña Colada is a popular, important, and good drink. The most important aspect in making the best Piña Colada is the cream of coconut or Piña Colada mix. (We import from Mexico Collins Piña Colada Mix and Coco Collins Cream. Both are made from fresh coconuts and are canned in Mexico to our specifications.)

A Piña Colada mix is usually a cream of coconut already combined with the pineapple juice. (Thus, when using Collins Piña Colada Mix, you merely add the rum.)

Tips

I believe that it is a little more difficult to use your own pineapple juice, but it is worth it. I also recommend Coco Lopez in a can, and I think Holland House Coco Casa in bottles is also excellent. I suggest that you experiment.

If the cream of coconut is hard or has solidified in the can, merely put it under hot tap water for 5 minutes and it should return to solution. It is all right to blend the solidified mixture.

Never store cream of coconut in the can after it is opened. Put it into a plastic container and refrigerate.

Also, make sure the ice is totally blended and ingredients are frothy. There should be no ice at all when the blender stops.

(A Chi-Chi is made merely by substituting vodka for the rum.)

Strawberry Colada—Add 4 fresh or frozen strawberries and ½ oz. strawberry liqueur.

PINK LADY

1½ oz. gin
¾ oz. lime juice
Dash grenadine
Dash sweet cream
Dash lemon juice

In a shaker combine ingredients with crushed ice. Shake well and strain into a prechilled cocktail glass.

PINK SQUIRREL

1 oz. crème de noyaux
1 oz. white crème de cacao
1 oz. cream

Combine ingredients in a blender or shaker filled with ice. Shake or blend well and then strain into a prechilled cocktail glass. No garnish.

PLANTER'S PUNCH

1½ oz. dark rum
2 oz. orange juice
¾ oz. lemon juice
½ oz. lime juice
¼ teaspoon grenadine

Blend or shake ingredients with cracked ice and pour into a tall Collins glass. Garnish with an orange slice and cherry.

PRESBYTERIAN, OR PRES

1½ oz. whiskey
Club soda
Ginger ale

Fill a highball glass with ice and pour in the whiskey. Fill the remainder of the glass with equal amounts of ginger ale and club soda. Garnish with a lemon twist.

PUPPY'S NOSE

½ oz. peppermint schnapps
½ oz. Tia Maria
½ oz. Irish cream

Using a shot glass, pour in the schnapps and Tia Maria. Float Irish cream on top. No chilling or stirring. Drink named because it looks like a Puppy's nose.

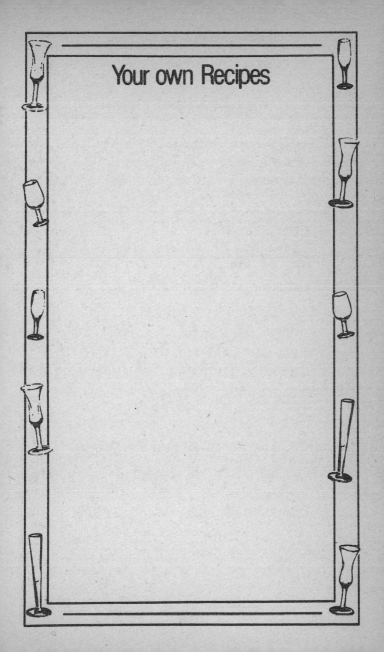

Your own Recipes

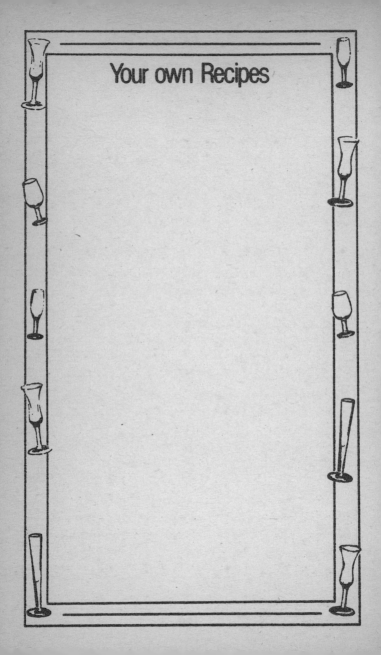

Your own Recipes

R

RABBIT

1½ oz. Southern Comfort
¼ oz. peppermint schnapps

In a shot glass pour the chilled Southern Comfort and float the peppermint schnapps.

RAMOS GIN FIZZ

1 oz. gin
1 egg white
½ oz. Orange Flower Water
½ oz. cream
1 teaspoon sugar (superfine)
Club soda

Put all the ingredients except club soda into a blender with a cup of ice. Strain into a prechilled parfait glass or large stemmed glass. Fill with club soda and stir very gently.

RASPBERRY CREAM

1 oz. vodka
¾ oz. Chambourd
¾ oz. cream

Fill a rocks glass with ice. Add the vodka and Chambourd. Then float the cream on top.

RED HOT

1 oz. cinnamon schnapps
3 drops Tabasco sauce

Add the ingredients in a shot glass and stir.

ROB ROY

1½ oz. Scotch
¼–½ oz. sweet vermouth
Dash Angostura bitters (optional)

Make this the same as a Martini, either in a rocks or cocktail glass. Fill a rocks glass with ice and add the vermouth and Scotch. Stir gently.

For a straight-up, take ingredients and put into a shaker with cracked ice. Shake and strain into a prechilled cocktail glass. Garnish with a cherry or olive.

ROB ROY—DRY

1½ oz. Scotch
¼–½ oz. dry vermouth
Dash of Angostura bitters (optional)

Make this the same way as Rob Roy above. To make an extra dry Rob Roy, merely cut down on the vermouth.

ROB ROY—PERFECT

1½ oz. Scotch
¼ oz. sweet vermouth
¼ oz. dry vermouth
Dash of Angostura bitters (optional)

Make this the same way as a Rob Roy above.

ROOT BEER

¾ oz. Galliano
¾ oz. vodka
½ oz. cola

Shake with ice and strain into a shot glass.

ROSEBUD

1½ oz. gin
½ teaspoon Rose's lime juice
Tonic water

Fill a tall Collins glass with ice. Add gin and Rose's and stir. Fill with tonic water and garnish with a lime wedge.

RUM BLACK RUSSIAN

1½ oz. light rum
¾ oz. Kahlúa or coffee liqueur

Fill a rocks glass with ice. Add ingredients. Stir.

RUM AND COLA

2 oz. dark rum
Cola

Pour the rum over ice cubes in a Collins glass. Fill the glass with cola and stir gently. Garnish with a lime wedge.

RUM AND DIET COLA

1½ oz. Bacardi light rum
Diet cola

Pour the rum over ice cubes in Collins glass. Fill the glass with diet cola and stir gently. Garnish with a lime wedge. This recipe has fewer calories than 5 oz. of white wine and less alcohol by volume.

RUM COLLINS

1½ oz. dark rum
¾ oz. lemon juice
Dash of lime juice
Club soda

Mix the rum and lemon and lime juice together in a shaker filled with cracked ice. Shake well and strain into a Collins glass. Top with club soda and stir gently. A sweet-sour premix should be used instead of lemon and lime juice. Garnish with a lime wedge and cherry. Provide short straws.

RUM GIMLET

1½ oz. light rum
½ oz. Rose's lime juice

Fill a cocktail shaker with ice. Add ingredients and shake. Strain into a prechilled cocktail glass with a lime wedge as a garnish.

To serve on the rocks, shake and pour into a rocks glass with ice cubes. Garnish with a lime wedge.

RUM SCREWDRIVER

1½ oz. rum
Orange juice

Fill a Collins glass with ice and add rum. Fill with orange juice and stir.

RUM SOUR

1½ oz. rum
3 oz. lemon juice
Dash of bar foamer

Blend or shake with 1 cup of cracked ice. Pour into an old-fashioned glass or strain into a stemmed glass. All the ingredients, except the rum, should be replaced with a sweet-sour premix. Garnish with a lime wedge. To make a stone sour, reduce the lemon juice by half and add 1 oz. orange juice. (A better way is to use Collins Stone Sour Mix with the rum.)

RUM AND TONIC

1½ oz. light rum
Tonic water

Fill a Collins glass with ice. Add rum and fill with tonic water. Stir and garnish with a lime wedge.

RUSSIAN COCKTAIL

1 oz. vodka
1 oz. gin
1 oz. white crème de cacao

Pour over ice in an old-fashioned glass. Stir well. It can be made straight up by adding ingredients in a shaker with ice. Strain into a cocktail glass.

RUSSIAN QUAALUDE

¼ oz. vodka
¼ oz. Bailey's Irish Cream
¼ oz. Frangelico
¼ oz. amaretto

Pour all ingredients into a shot glass and stir. This can also be served on the rocks in a rocks glass with ice.

RUSTY NAIL

1 oz. Scotch
¾ oz. Drambuie

Fill a rocks glass with ice and add ingredients. Stir. No garnish.

Your own Recipes

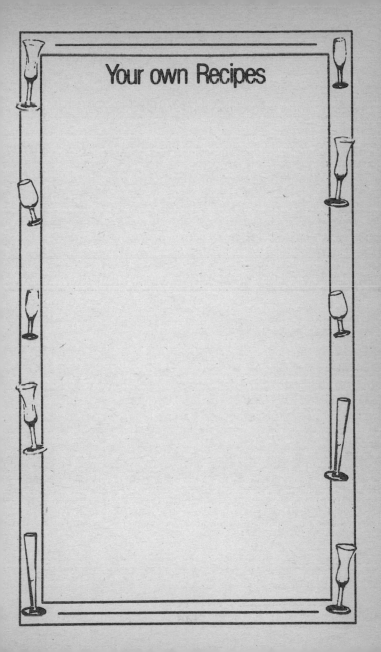

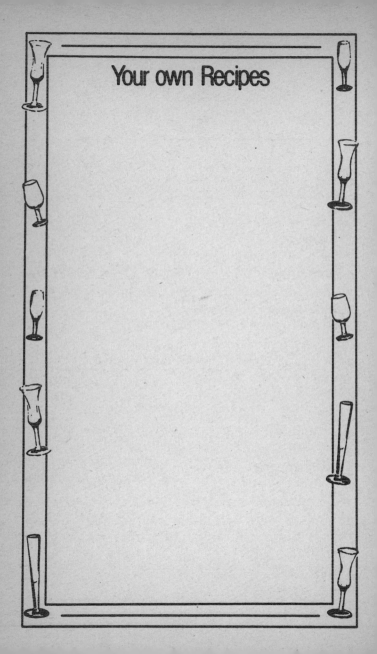

Your own Recipes

S

SALTY DOG

1½ oz. vodka and gin
Grapefruit juice

*Salt the rim of a highball glass. Fill the glass with
ice and add the vodka or gin. Fill with the grapefruit
juice and stir. No garnish.*

SANGRIA (by the gallon)

2 liters Burgundy wine
1 liter rosé
6 oz. brandy
6 oz. sweetened lemon juice
20 oz. orange juice

*Pour all ingredients into a punch bowl and add
several cups of ice cubes and stir well. Float
orange slices, lime wedges, and cherries on top.*

SCARLETT O'HARA

1½ oz. Southern Comfort
½ oz. lime juice
Dash grenadine

*Use a mixing glass and stir ingredients with ice.
Strain into a prechilled cocktail glass.*

SCOTCH MIST

1½ oz. Scotch

*A "mist" merely denotes crushed ice. Thus, a
Scotch Mist means Scotch with crushed ice. Pour
the Scotch into a glass with crushed ice, and you
can garnish with a lemon twist.*

SCOTCH AND SODA

1½ oz. Scotch
Club soda

*Pour Scotch over ice cubes in an old-fashioned
glass. Fill with soda and stir gently. Can be garnished
with a lemon twist.*

SCOTCH SOUR

1½ oz. Scotch
2 oz. sweetened lemon juice

Blend or shake with 1 cup of cracked ice. Pour into an old-fashioned glass or strain into a cocktail glass. (I recommend replacing the lemon juice with a sweet-sour premix with a foamy head.)

For a Scotch Stone Sour, add 1 oz. orange juice and a dash of sugar.

SCREAMING ORGASM

¾ oz. vodka
¾ oz. Kahlúa
¾ oz. Bailey's Irish Cream
¾ oz. amaretto

Blend ingredients with ice and pour into a prechilled rocks glass. For a straight-up, strain the contents of blender into a prechilled cocktail glass. No garnish. If the amaretto is left out, the drink is called an Orgasm.

SCREWDRIVER

1½ oz. vodka
Orange juice

Fill a highball glass with ice and add the vodka. Fill with orange juice and stir. No garnish.

SEA BREEZE

1½ oz. vodka
1½ oz. cranberry juice
1½ oz. grapefruit juice

Fill a highball glass with ice and add ingredients. Stir. No garnish.

SEVEN AND SEVEN

1½ oz. blended whiskey
7-Up

Pour the blended whiskey over ice in an old-fashioned or highball glass. Fill with 7-Up and stir very gently. No garnish.

SHERRY FLIP

1½ oz. sherry wine
1 whole egg
1 teaspoon sugar
Nutmeg

In a blender ½ filled with ice, add the sherry, egg, and sugar. Blend well and strain into a large wine or cocktail glass. Sprinkle nutmeg on top of the drink.

SIDECAR

1 oz. brandy
½ oz. Triple Sec or Cointreau
1 oz. lime juice
1 egg white

Shake well with cracked ice and strain into a large cocktail or wineglass. Coat the rim of the glass with sugar by inverting the empty glass and covering the rim with lime juice and dipping into sugar.

SILVER BULLET

1½ oz. gin
Splash of Scotch

To make it on the rocks, fill a rocks glass with ice and add ingredients. To make it straight up, chill a cocktail glass. Fill a shaker with ice, add ingredients, stir, and strain into the prechilled cocktail glass. No garnish.

To make a Vodka Silver Bullet, substitute vodka for the gin. No garnish.

SILVER FIZZ

1 oz. lemon juice
1½ oz. gin
White of one egg
1 teaspoon sugar

Shake well and pour into a Collins glass over ice. Top with a splash of club soda and stir gently.

SINGAPORE SLING

1 oz. gin
¾ oz. cherry brandy
½ oz. grenadine
2 oz. sweetened lemon juice
Dash Angostura bitters
Club soda

Take all ingredients except club soda and shake with one cup of ice. Pour into a large stemmed glass and top with a splash of soda. Garnish with an orange slice and a cherry.

SKYRIDE (from the 1933 Chicago World's Fair)

1½ oz. gin
1 oz. lemon juice
4 dashes grenadine
1 oz. cream

Shake well and pour into a large highball glass with ice.

SLAMMER, Adam's or A.C.'s

¾ oz. vodka
¾ oz. 7-Up

Pour the vodka into a shot glass. Float the 7-Up. Cover the top of the shot glass with a napkin and carefully and quickly pound the glass and immediately drink. Be careful you do not break the glass and injure yourself.

SLAMMER, Elizabeth's

¾ oz. gin
¾ oz. 7-Up or Squirt

Pour the gin into a shot glass. Next float the 7-Up or Squirt on top. Put your palm over the top of the shot glass and carefully, so you do not break the glass and injure yourself, pound the glass onto the table. Drink immediately. Instead of your palm, a napkin can be substituted.

SLAMMER, Helene's

¾ oz. bourbon
¾ oz. 7-Up

Pour the bourbon into a shot glass. Float the 7-Up on top of the bourbon. Carefully, so as not to break the glass or injure yourself, place your hand over the top of the shot glass and slam the drink onto the bar. This drink will have a fizz on top. Drink immediately.

SLAMMER, Howard's

¾ oz. rum
¾ oz. cola

Pour the rum into a shot glass. Float the cola on top of the rum. Immediately put your hand over the top of the shot glass and pound the shot glass twice onto the bar or table. The drink will have a fizz on top. Drink at once. Be careful you do not break the glass or injure yourself.

SLAMMER, Susan's

¾ oz. tequila
¾ oz. 7-Up

Put the tequila into a shot glass. Float the 7-Up. Cover the top of the shot glass with the palm of your hand and carefully pound on a hard surface. A fizz will appear on the drink. Consume immediately. Be careful.

SLIPPERY KNOB

1½ oz. vodka
Splash of Grand Marnier

This is made exactly like a Martini. See Martini for directions for straight up or on the rocks.

SLOE COMFORTABLE SCREW

1 oz. Southern Comfort
1 oz. Sloe gin
Orange juice

Fill a rocks glass with ice and add ingredients. Stir well and serve. Vary the amount of orange juice to your personal taste.

SLOE GIN FIZZ

1½ oz. sloe gin
1 oz. lemon juice (sweetened)
Club soda

Combine the sloe gin and lemon juice in a blender with ice. (The lemon juice should be replaced by a sweet-sour premix.) Blend and pour into a Collins glass. Only fill to within ½ inch of top. Fill with club soda for fizz. Stir gently. No garnish.

SLOE SCREW

1–1½ oz. sloe gin
Orange juice

Fill a prechilled highball glass with ice and add the sloe gin and fill with orange juice. Stir and serve. No garnish. Also called a Sloe Screwdriver.

SMITH & KERNS

1 oz. dark crème de cacao
2 oz. cream or half-and-half
Club soda

Fill a highball glass with ice and add first two ingredients. Stir and add a splash of club soda.

SNOWSHOE

1 oz. brandy
1 oz. peppermint schnapps

Pour the brandy and schnapps into a brandy snifter. Swirl to mix and serve.

SOMBRERO

1½ oz. coffee liqueur or Tia Maria
¾ oz. half-and-half

Pour the liqueur into an ice-filled rocks glass or an empty pony glass and float the cream on top of the liqueur, using an inverted spoon. See Tips for floating cream.

SOUTHERN COMFORT MANHATTAN

1½ oz. Southern Comfort
¼–½ oz. dry vermouth
Dash of Angostura bitters

To make it on the rocks, fill a rocks glass with ice. Add vermouth, Angostura bitters, and Southern Comfort. To make it straight up, begin by chilling a cocktail glass. Then fill a shaker with ice and add ingredients. Stir and strain into the prechilled cocktail glass. Garnish with a cherry.

SPRITZER

White wine
Club soda

Fill a tall glass with ice. Pour white wine until it fills ½ of the glass. Fill with club soda and garnish with a slice of lime.

STINGER

1½ oz. brandy
¾ oz. white crème de menthe

To make it on the rocks, pour into an ice-filled rocks glass and stir.

To make it straight up, chill a cocktail glass. Place ingredients in a shaker with cracked ice and shake. Strain into the prechilled cocktail glass. No garnish.

STRAWBERRY SHORTCAKE, Andrea's

1½ oz. strawberry liqueur
½ oz. cream
Whipped cream

In a rocks glass filled with ice, add the strawberry liqueur. Float the cream on top of the liqueur using an inverted spoon. Top with whipped cream and garnish with a cherry.

SUIZESS

1½ oz. Pernod
1 teaspoon superfine sugar
White of 1 egg

Shake well and pour into a prechilled cocktail glass. Serve club soda on the side.

SWEET PEACH

¾ oz. amaretto
¾ oz. peach schnapps
½ oz. orange juice

Shake ingredients with ice and strain into a shot glass.

Your own Recipes

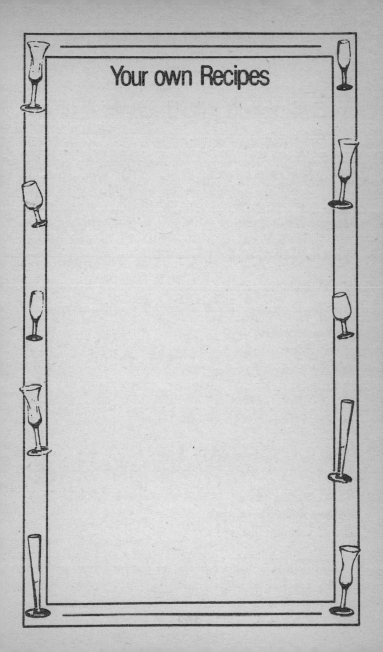

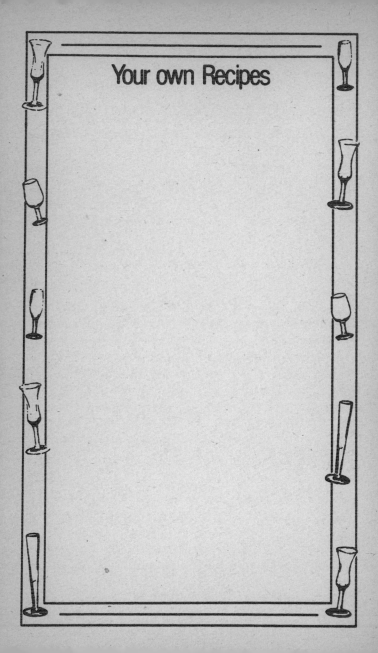

Your own Recipes

T

TAFFY APPLE

1½ oz. rum
Large tablespoon hot buttered rum mix
Hot apple cider

Put the rum in a coffee mug. Then add the hot buttered rum mix. Then fill the mug with hot apple cider. If you do not want to use a hot buttered rum premix, I provide a scratch recipe in this book under Hot Buttered Rum.

TEQUILA SLAMMER

1½ oz. tequila
7-Up

Use a 2 oz. shot glass. Put the tequila in first. Then float the 7-Up. Then carefully and quickly place a napkin over the shot glass and slam the contents down. Drink immediately. Be careful that you do not break the glass and injure yourself.

TEQUILA SUNRISE

1 oz. tequila
Orange juice
½ oz. grenadine

Fill a Collins glass with ice. Pour in the tequila and fill the glass with orange juice. Stir and add the grenadine.

THIS AND THAT

1 oz. Grand Marnier
1 oz. cognac

Pour ingredients into a brandy snifter. No garnish.

TINY DANCER

¾ oz. vodka
¾ oz. Frangelico
¾ Cuarenta y Tres ("43")

In a rocks glass filled with ice, add ingredients and stir. No garnish.

TOM COLLINS

1½ oz. gin
1½ oz. sweetened lemon juice
Club soda

The lemon juice should be replaced by a sweet-sour premix. Blend or shake the gin and lemon juice with cracked ice. Pour into a Collins glass and top with club soda and garnish with an orange slice and cherry.

Brandy Collins—Substitute brandy for gin.
John Collins—Substitute whiskey for gin.
Rum Collins—Substitute rum for gin.
Vodka Collins—Substitute vodka for gin.

TOOTSIE ROLL

½ oz. Kahlúa
1½ oz. dark crème de cacao
¾ oz. orange juice

Fill a cocktail shaker with cracked ice. Add ingredients and stir. Prechill a shot glass. Strain from shaker into the shot glass. No garnish.

TORPEDO

This is a mini-Bloody Mary cut down to a shot glass. Follow Bloody Mary recipe and cut down to shot-glass size.

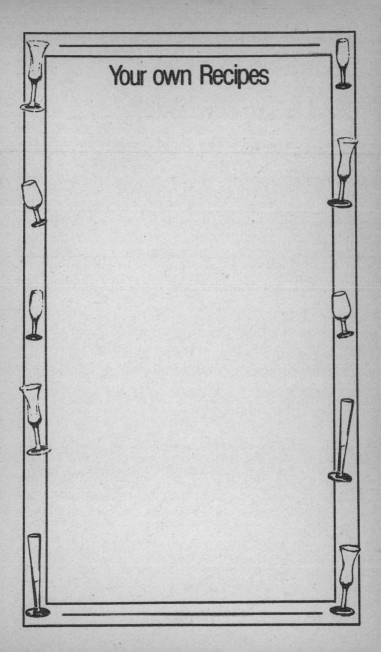

Your own Recipes

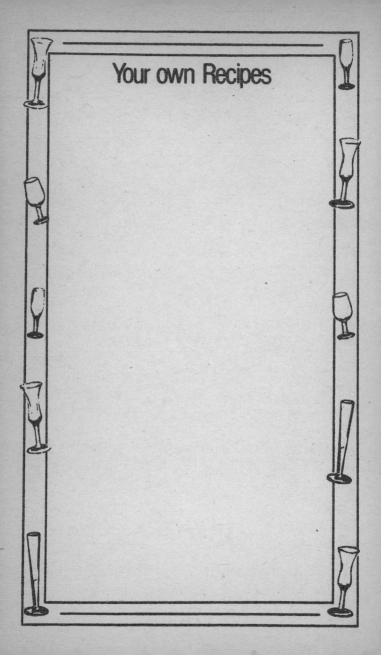

Your own Recipes

V

VANILLA COKE

1½ oz. Cuarenta y Tres ("43")
Cola

Fill a highball glass with ice and add "43" (Cuarenta y Tres). Then fill with cola.

VERMOUTH CASSIS

1½ oz. dry vermouth
½ teaspoon crème de cassis
Club soda

Prechill a wineglass. Add vermouth and cassis and stir. Top with club soda and garnish with a lemon twist.

VIRGIN MARY

A Bloody Mary without any alcohol. See recipe under Bloody Mary, but do not add liquor.

VODKA COLLINS

A Tom Collins substituting vodka for gin. See recipe under Tom Collins.

VODKA GIBSON

This is a Martini substituting vodka for gin, and the garnish is a cocktail onion.

VODKA GIMLET

See recipe for Gimlet, substituting vodka for gin.

VODKA SLING

1 oz. vodka
½ oz. Benedictine
½ oz. cherry brandy
1 oz. lemon juice
Dash Angostura bitters

Pour ingredients in a shaker and strain into a Collins glass. Add club soda and garnish with an orange and cherry.

VODKA SOUR

1½ oz. vodka
1 oz. sweetened lemon juice

Blend or shake with 1 cup of cracked ice. Pour into an old-fashioned glass or strain into a cocktail glass. Garnish with an orange slice. (The sweetened lemon juice can be and probably should be replaced by a sweet-sour ready mix such as Collins Sweet Sour. A ready mix will also give a foamy head to a drink.) Unsweetened lemon juice can also be used, depending upon your taste.

VODKA STONE SOUR

1½ oz. vodka
1 oz. sweetened lemon juice
1½ oz. orange juice

Blend or shake with 1 cup of cracked ice. Pour into an old-fashioned glass or strain into a cocktail glass. Garnish with an orange slice and a cherry. (This recipe can be changed to unsweetened lemon juice or a sweet-sour ready mix or Collins Stone Sour. Again, a premix should contain a foaming ingredient for a foamy head on the drink.)

VODKA AND TONIC

1½ oz. vodka
Tonic

Fill a highball glass with ice. Add vodka and top with tonic. Stir and garnish with a lime wedge.

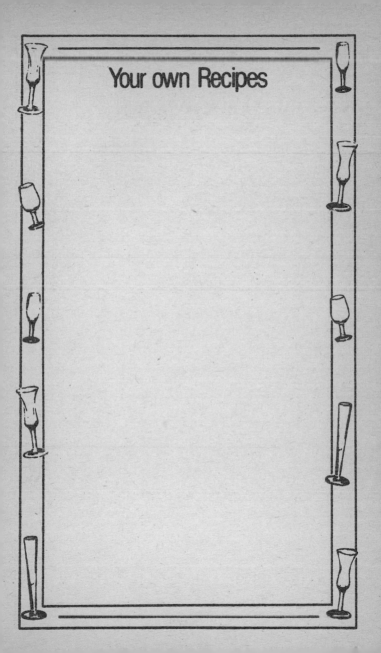

Your own Recipes

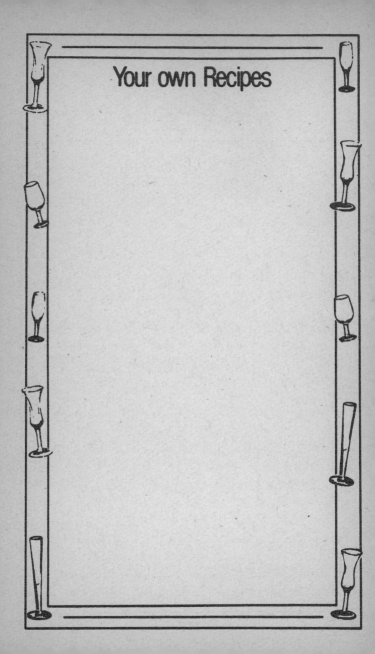

Your own Recipes

W

WATERMELON

1 oz. strawberry liqueur
1 oz. vodka
Dash Triple Sec
Dash lime juice
1 oz. orange juice

Fill a cocktail shaker with ice and add ingredients, shake and strain into a shot glass or into an ice-filled rocks glass. Color should be like a ripe watermelon.

WHISKEY SOUR

1½ oz. whiskey
1½ oz. sweetened lemon juice
Egg white

Blend the ingredients with ice and pour into a rocks glass or strain into a cocktail glass. (The lemon juice and egg white should be replaced by a sweet-sour premix.)

WHISKEY STONE SOUR

1½ oz. whiskey
¾ oz. sweetened lemon juice
½ oz. orange juice

Blend or shake with 1 cup of cracked ice. Pour into an old-fashioned glass or strain into a cocktail glass. Garnish with an orange slice and a cherry. (This recipe can be changed to unsweetened lemon juice or a sweet-sour ready mix or even a Collins Stone Sour. Again, a premix should contain a foaming ingredient for a foamy head on drink.)

WHITE LADY

1 oz. Cointreau
½ oz. white crème de menthe
½ oz. brandy

Pour over ice, stir, and serve.

WHITE RUSSIAN

1½ oz. vodka
¾ oz. Kahlúa
¾ oz. cream

Fill a rocks glass with ice and add vodka and Kahlúa. Next, float the cream on top (pg. xxvi). See Tips for floating cream.

WINE COOLER

Fill a Collins glass with ice. Fill the glass ⅔ with wine and fill with 7-Up. Garnish with a lime wedge.

WINE SPRITZER

Chablis, Rhine, or rosé wine
Club soda

Pour wine into an iced Collins glass. Two-thirds of the glass should be filled with the wine. The last ⅓ of the glass is for the club soda. Stir very gently and add a lime wedge as a garnish.

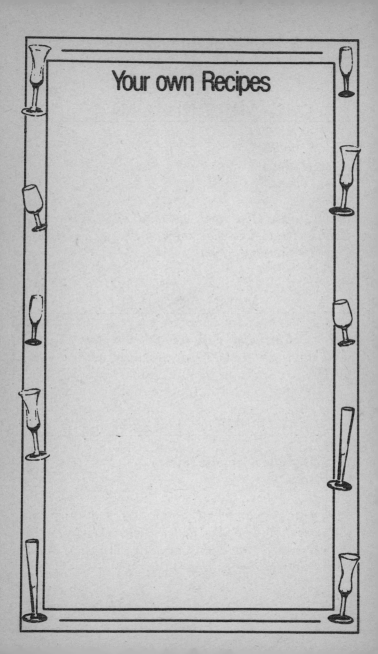

Your own Recipes

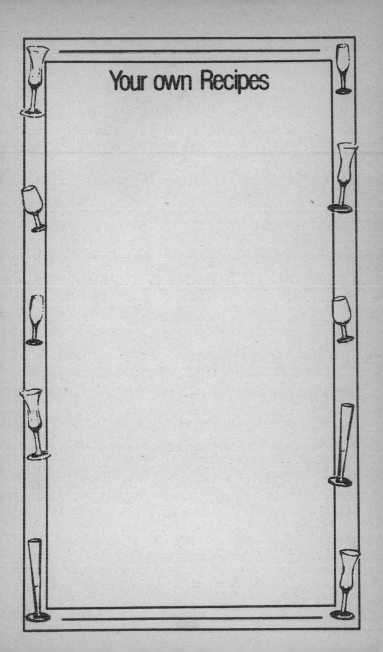

Your own Recipes

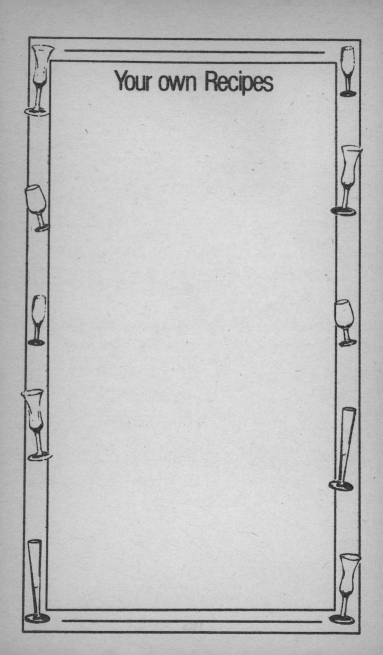

Your own Recipes

Z

ZOMBIE

¾ oz. light rum
¾ oz. dark rum
¾ oz. Gold Rum (or highest proof available)
1 oz. sweetened lemon juice
½ oz. cherry brandy

Blend the rums and lemon juice together with ice.
Strain into a Collins glass with 2 cubes of ice.
Float the cherry brandy on top.

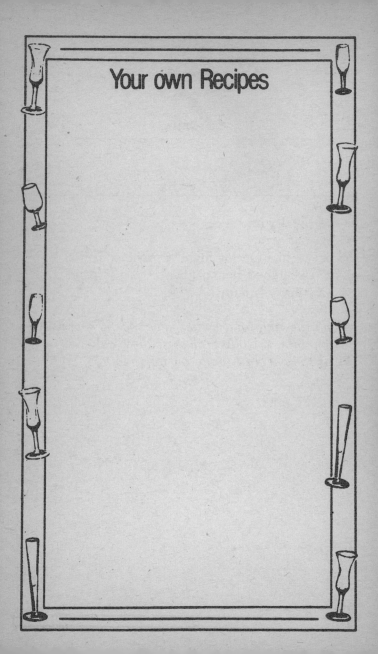

Your own Recipes

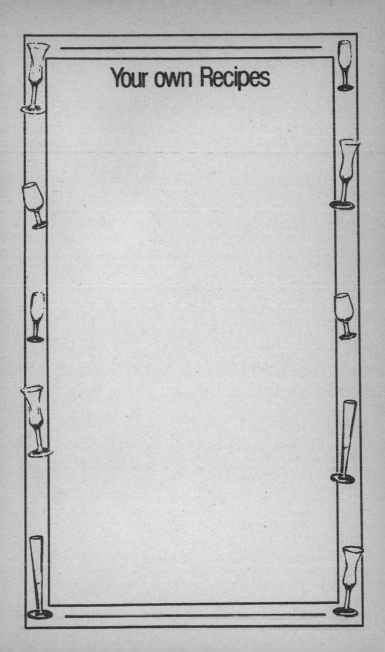

Your own Recipes

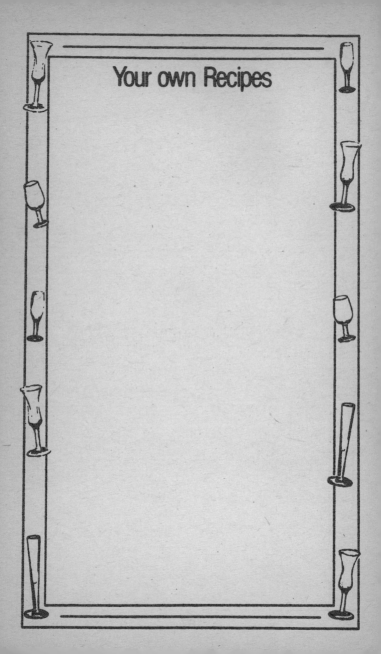

Your own Recipes

AMARETTO DRINKS

Alabama Slammer
Almond Colada
Almond Mocha
Amaretto and Cream
Amaretto Sour
Amaretto Stone Sour
B.J.
Banshee—Super
Blood Clot

French Connection
Godfather
Godmother
Italian Coffee
Kool-Aid
Orgasm—Screaming
Russian Quaalude
Sweet Peach

APRICOT BRANDY DRINKS

Apricot Cider
Apricot Sour
Apricot Stone Sour

Bun Warmer
Mai Tai II

BOURBON DRINKS

Alabama Slammer
Bourbon Sour
Collins

Godfather
Mint Julep
Slammer, Helene's

BRANDY DRINKS

Apple Toddy
Apricot Cider
Apricot Sour
Apricot Stone Sour
B&B
Between the Sheets
Brandy Alexander
Brandy Cider
Brandy Cocktail
Brandy Collins
Brandy Fizz
Brandy Flip
Brandy Ice
Brandy Manhattan
Brandy Old Fashioned
Brandy Sour
Brandy Stone Sour
Brave Bull
Café Royal

Champagne Punch I
Champagne Sunset
Coffee Royal
Collins
Eggnog—Baltimore
Eggnog—Brandy
Fizz
French 75
Glogg
Hot Toddy
Keoke Coffee I
Keoke Coffee II
Manhattan—Brandy
Old Fashioned—
    Wisconsin
Sidecar
Snowshoe
Stinger
White Lady

CHAMPAGNE DRINKS

Black Velvet
Champagne Berry
Champagne Cocktail
Champagne Punch I
Champagne Punch II

Champagne Sunset
French 75
Kir Royal
Mimosa—Standard
Mimosa—Special

COGNAC

B-52
Between the Sheets II

French Connection
This and That

COFFEE LIQUEUR DRINKS

Black Russian
Coffee Hummer
Colorado Bulldog
Hummer
Keoke Coffee II

Orgasm
Orgasm—Screaming
Rum Black Russian
Sombrero

GALLIANO DRINKS

Freddy Fuddpucker
Golden Cadillac
Golden Russian

Harvey Wallbanger
Root Beer

GIN DRINKS

Abbey
Abby Cocktail
Alabama Fizz
Alexander
Bloody Mary
Boxcar
Clover Club
Collins
Dry Martini
Dubonnet Cocktail
Fizz
French 75
Gibson
Gimlet
Gin Buck
Gin Fizz
Gin and It
Gin Rickey
Gin Sour
Gin Stone Sour

Gin and Tonic
Long Island Iced Tea
Martini—Standard
Martini—Extra Dry
Martini, Scotty's
Martini, Tom Carney's
Negroni
Orange Blossom
Pimm's Cup
Pink Lady
Ramos Gin Fizz
Rosebud
Russian Cocktail
Salty Dog
Silver Bullet
Silver Fizz
Singapore Sling
Skyride
Slammer, Elizabeth's
Tom Collins

IRISH CREAM DRINKS

B-52
Deep T
Down Under
Dreamsicle
Eggnog—Irish
Fritz's Coffee

Irish Delight
Orgasm
Orgasm—Screaming
Puppy's Nose
Russian Quaalude

IRISH WHISKEY DRINKS

Down Under
Irish Coffee

Irish Delight

KAHLÚA DRINKS

Angels Tip
B.J.
B-52
Black Russian
Coffee Hummer
Colorado Bulldog
Deep T
Down Under
Hummer
Irish Coffee
Jamaican Coffee

Kahlúa and Cream
Kahlúa Hummer
Keoke Coffee I
Keoke Coffee II
Mexican Coffee II
Orgasm
Orgasm—Screaming
Rum Black Russian
Tootsie Roll
White Russian

MIDORI DRINKS

Alligator	Midori Sour
Melon Ball	Midori Stone Sour

RUM DRINKS

Acapulco	Jamaican Coffee
Bacardi Cocktail	Kahlúa Hummer
Banana Colada	Keoke Coffee I
Banana Daiquiri	Long Island Iced Tea
Coconut Rum	Mai Tai I
Coffee Hummer	Mai Tai II
Cuba Libre	Mai Tai III
Collins	Mary Pickford
Daiquiri—Banana	Piña Colada
Daiquiri—Coconut	Planter's Punch
Daiquiri—Peach	Rum Black Russian
Daiquiri—Raspberry	Rum and Cola
Daiquiri—Strawberry	Rum and Diet Cola
Eggnog—Bahamian	Rum Collins
Eggnog—Baltimore	Rum Gimlet
Eggnog—Brandy or Rum	Rum Screwdriver
Eggnog—Irish	Rum Sour
Fizz	Rum and Tonic
Green Lizard	Slammer, Howard's
Hot Buttered Rum	Taffy Apple
Hummer	Zombie

SCOTCH DRINKS

Dry Rob Roy
Godfather
Mamie Taylor
Perfect Rob Roy
Rob Roy
Rob Roy Dry

Rusty Nail
Scotch Mist
Scotch and Soda
Scotch Sour
Silver Bullet

SOUTHERN COMFORT DRINKS

Alabama Comfort
Blood Clot
Bun Warmer
Champagne Punch II
Eggnog—Southern
   Comfort
Georgia Peach

Kool-Aid
Rabbit
Scarlett O'Hara
Sloe Comfortable Screw
Southern Comfort
   Manhattan

TEQUILA DRINKS

Bloody Maria
Fizz
Freddy Fuddpucker
Long Island Iced Tea

Margarita
Slammer, Susan's
Tequila Slammer
Tequila Sunrise

VODKA DRINKS

Almond Colada
Black Russian
Bloody Bull
Bloody Mary
Bullshot
Cape Codder
Chi Chi
Collins
Colorado Bulldog
Deep T
Dry Martini
Fizz
Gibson
Gimlet
Godmother
Golden Russian
Greyhound
Harvey Wallbanger
Kamikaze
Kool-Aid
Long Island Iced Tea
Martini—Standard
Martini—Extra Dry

Melon Ball
Moscow Mule
Orgasm
Orgasm—Screaming
Raspberry Cream
Root Beer
Russian Cocktail
Russian Quaalude
Salty Dog
Screwdriver
Sea Breeze
Slammer, Adam's
Slippery Knob
Tiny Dancer
Vodka Collins
Vodka Gimlet
Vodka Sling
Vodka Sour
Vodka Stone Sour
Vodka and Tonic
Watermelon
White Russian

WHISKEY DRINKS

Boilermaker
Hot Toddy
John Collins
Manhattan
Manhattan—Dry
Manhattan—Perfect
Manhattan—Wisconsin

Old Fashioned—Standard
Old Fashioned, Tom
  Carney's
Presbyterian
Seven and Seven
Whiskey Sour
Whiskey Stone Sour